Billboard.

TOP 1000 SINGLES
1955 - 1990

HLP. Hal Leonard Publishing Corporation

7777 West Bluemound Road P.O. Box 13819 Milwaukee, WI 53213

Library of Congress Cataloging-in-Publication Data

Whitburn, Joel.
    Billboard top 1000 singles, 1955-1990: the 1000 biggest hits of the rock
    era/compiled by Joel Whitburn.
        p. cm.
    Rev. ed. of: Billboard top 1000 singles, 1955-1987. c1988.
    ISBN 0-7935-0347-7: $8.95
    1. Popular music—United States—Discography. 2. Popular music—United
    States—Statistics. I. Billboard. II. Title. III. Title: Top 1000 singles, 1955-1990.
    ML156.4.P6W454 1991
    016.78242164'026'6—dc20   91-10286
                                                                        CIP
                                                                         MN

Hal Leonard Publishing Corporation

7777 West Bluemound Road P.O. Box 13819 Milwaukee, WI 53213

CONTENTS

Displayed throughout this book are intriguing reproductions of the original full page
ads and reviews which appeared in Billboard magazine during the Sixties. The
previous edition of *Top 1000 Singles* featured ads and reviews from the Fifties and
our next edition will likely highlight the Seventies.

AUTHOR'S NOTE

If you could travel in a time machine back to 1954 and ask a 15-year-old kid to hum the melody of "The Wedding Of The Painted Doll," chances are you'd get a blank stare. "The Wedding Of The Painted Doll" by Leo Reisman was at the top of the pop charts for four weeks in 1929. Like teenagers today, a quarter of a century past is an eternity. Most of the popular songs of that pre-Depression era would belong only to that generation.

Ask a 15-year-old kid today, to sing the chorus of "Yesterday" by The Beatles (popular in 1965), and the kid might not cooperate, but he would know the exact tune you were talking about.

For whatever social and cultural reasons, the great pop hits of the rock era have withstood the test of time. Many of the tunes popular since the 1955 dawn of rock 'n' roll are currently on the airwaves. They resurface through play in films, television commercials and re-makes by other artists. Adults who, as teens, first heard the debuts of these now-oldies have not forgotten their favorites. The large number of oldies stations refresh their memories.

The titles within this book are many of the hits which have not been lost to other decades. In tribute to the greatest hits of the rock era, here is *Billboard's Top 1000*. Three and one-half decades of chart-topping hits are ranked within. For the first time, we have included a special listing of the 40 highest-ranking hits of each decade.

Have fun with this edition. Check out if "Venus" outshined "Moonglow," if "Mack The Knife" stuck it to "Stagger Lee," or if "Billie Jean" was more loved than "Maggie May."

These are the hits that have weathered the glacier of time. Thirty-five years have rearranged the musical landscape but the staying power of these classics remains unchanged.

JOEL WHITBURN

THE RANKING SYSTEM

The ranking methodology used to cover these 36 years of hits is a logical and simple one based on the principle that the highest position at which a record peaks is the single most important factor during its chart life. Climbing its way to the upper echelons of the chart is a battle each hit record wages in the never-ending race for chart superiority. And when its chart life is over, the position at which it peaked is the key statistic reflected upon by music professionals and is also the primary statistic used in the rankings for this book. Simply put, all #1 records will be ranked above records that peaked at #2.

This *Top 1000* ranking includes every record that peaked at position #1 plus over 60% of the records that peaked at #2, beginning with the July 9, 1955 chart and ending with the September 22, 1990 *Hot 100* chart.

Following is the chronology used in ranking the *Top 1000* hits:

1) Peak position

   a) All records peaking at #1 are listed first, followed by records peaking at #2.

   b) Ties among each highest position grouping are broken in the following order:

2) Total weeks record held its peak position

3) Total weeks charted in the Top 10

4) Total weeks charted in the Top 40

5) Total weeks charted

If there are still ties, a computerized inverse point system is used to calculate a point total for each record based on its weekly chart positions. For each week a record appears on the charts it is given points based on its chart position for that week (#1=100 points, #2=99 points, etc.). These points are added together to create a raw point total for each record, which is used to break any remaining ties.

The *BILLBOARD* charts were used exclusively in compiling this data. For the years 1955-1958, the following *Billboard* pop charts were researched, with each record's highest position taken from whichever chart it attained a higher ranking: *Top 100, Best Sellers, Most Played by Jockeys* and *Most Played in Juke Boxes.* From August of 1958 to the present, the sole all-encompassing pop chart used was *Billboard's Hot 100 Singles.*

THE RANKING

This section lists, in rank order, the *Top 1000* hits from 1955-1990. The **peak position** and the **total weeks at the peak position** are highlighted above each group of corresponding titles.

Columnar headings show the following data:

YR: Year record reached its peak position

WEEKS: 10 - Total weeks charted in the Top 10
40 - Total weeks charted in the Top 40
CH - Total weeks charted

RANK: *Top 1000* ranking (highlighted in dark type)

GOLD: ● - RIAA certified gold record (million seller)*
▲ - RIAA certified platinum record (two million seller)*

SYM (type of recording):

[I] Instrumental
[N] Novelty
[C] Comedy
[F] Foreign language
[X] Christmas
[S] Spoken word

TIME: Playing time of each record

A small check-off circle is provided next to each title to aid in keeping track of the *Top 1000* records in your collection.

The Recording Industry Association of America (RIAA) began certifying gold records in 1958 and platinum records in 1976. Prior to these dates, there are most certainly some hits that would have qualified for these certifications. Also, some record labels have never requested RIAA certifications for their hits. As of January 1, 1989, RIAA lowered the certification for gold singles to sales of 500,000 units and platinum to one million units.

DON'T BE CRUEL/ HOUND DOG

For 11 consecutive weeks (August 18, 1956-October 27, 1956) on the *Best Sellers* charts, and for 11 consecutive weeks (September 1, 1956-November 10, 1956) on the *Juke Box* charts, the biggest 2-sided single in history held down the #1 spot. During this period, both charts combined 2-sided hits into a single listing on the charts. In both cases, "Hound Dog" debuted as the top side, with 'Don't Be Cruel' listed later as the top side. Both sides were enormously strong, and it's logical to assume that each would have held the #1 spot for at least 8 to 9 weeks had they been released as separate singles. However, as a powerhouse dual single, and with *Billboard* alternating the side shown first, their combined total stay at #1 makes it the biggest charted single of the rock era.

YR	WEEKS			RANK	GOLD	PEAK POSITION	PEAK WEEKS	SYM	TIME	ARTIST
	CH	40	10							

Pos 1 — 11 Wks

YR	CH	40	10	RANK	GOLD	TITLE	TIME	ARTIST
56	28	24	21	1	O	Don't Be Cruel/	2:03	
						Hound Dog	2:15	Elvis Presley

Pos 1 — 10 Wks

56	26	22	17	2	O	Singing The Blues	2:23	Guy Mitchell
81	26	21	15	3	O ▲	Physical	3:43	Olivia Newton-John
77	25	21	14	4	O ▲	You Light Up My Life	3:35	Debby Boone

Pos 1 — 9 Wks

59	26	22	16	5	O	Mack The Knife	3:04	Bobby Darin
57	30	22	15	6	O	All Shook Up	1:58	Elvis Presley
81	26	20	14	7	O ●	Bette Davis Eyes	3:47	Kim Carnes
68	19	19	14	8	O ●	Hey Jude	7:11	The Beatles
81	27	19	13	9	O ▲	Endless Love	4:26	Diana Ross & Lionel Richie
60	21	17	12	10	O ●	The Theme From "A Summer Place" .... [I]	2:24	Percy Faith

Pos 1 — 8 Wks

55	38	25	19	11	O	Rock Around The Clock	2:08	Bill Haley & His Comets
56	37	22	16	12	O	The Wayward Wind	2:56	Gogi Grant
55	22	19	16	13	O	Sixteen Tons	2:34	"Tennessee" Ernie Ford
56	27	22	15	14	O	Heartbreak Hotel	2:06	Elvis Presley
83	22	20	13	15	O ●	Every Breath You Take	4:13	The Police
78	20	18	13	16	O ▲	Night Fever	3:32	Bee Gees
76	23	17	11	17	O ●	Tonight's The Night (Gonna Be Alright)	3:55	Rod Stewart

Pos 1 — 7 Wks

57	34	24	17	18	O	Love Letters In The Sand	2:12	Pat Boone
57	27	19	15	19	O	Jailhouse Rock	2:10	Elvis Presley
57	25	18	14	20	O	(Let Me Be Your) Teddy Bear	1:43	Elvis Presley
78	25	19	12	21	O ▲	Shadow Dancing	4:34	Andy Gibb
58	21	18	12	22	O	At The Hop	2:31	Danny & The Juniors
61	23	17	12	23	O	Tossin' And Turnin'	2:40	Bobby Lewis
82	20	16	12	24	O ▲	I Love Rock 'N Roll	2:45	Joan Jett & The Blackhearts
82	19	15	12	25	O ●	Ebony And Ivory	3:41	Paul McCartney/Stevie Wonder
64	15	14	12	26	O ●	I Want To Hold Your Hand	2:24	The Beatles
66	15	13	12	27	O ●	I'm A Believer	2:41	The Monkees
83	24	17	11	28	O ▲	Billie Jean	4:50	Michael Jackson
68	15	15	11	29	O	I Heard It Through The Grapevine	2:59	Marvin Gaye

Pos 1 — 6 Wks

55	21	21	17	30	O	Love Is A Many-Splendored Thing	2:56	Four Aces featuring Al Alberts
56	25	20	16	31	O	Rock And Roll Waltz	2:53	Kay Starr
56	24	20	16	32	O	The Poor People Of Paris .... [I]	2:24	Les Baxter
55	19	19	16	33	O	The Yellow Rose Of Texas	3:00	Mitch Miller
78	25	19	15	34	O ▲	Le Freak	3:30	Chic
56	24	19	15	35	O	Memories Are Made Of This	2:15	Dean Martin
82	25	18	15	36	O ▲	Eye Of The Tiger	3:45	Survivor
83	25	20	14	37	O ●	Flashdance...What A Feeling	3:55	Irene Cara
57	26	19	14	38	O	April Love	2:39	Pat Boone
80	25	19	13	39	O ●	Lady	3:51	Kenny Rogers
83	22	18	13	40	O ●	Say Say Say	3:55	Paul McCartney & Michael Jackson
59	21	18	13	41	O ●	The Battle Of New Orleans	2:33	Johnny Horton

YR	WEEKS			RANK	G O L D	PEAK POSITION		SYM	TIME	ARTIST
	CH	40	10							

Pos 1 6 Wks Cont'd

YR	CH	40	10	RANK	GOLD	PEAK POSITION	PEAK WEEKS	SYM	TIME	ARTIST
57	21	17	13	42	O	Young Love			2:24	Tab Hunter
82	25	20	12	43	O ●	Centerfold			3:35	The J. Geils Band
80	25	19	12	44	O ●	Call Me			3:30	Blondie
58	22	19	12	45	O	It's All In The Game			2:25	Tommy Edwards
79	22	16	12	46	O ●	My Sharona			3:58	The Knack
69	17	16	11	47	O ●	Aquarius/Let The Sunshine In			4:45	The 5th Dimension
72	18	15	11	48	O ●	The First Time Ever I Saw Your Face			4:15	Roberta Flack
72	18	15	11	49	O ●	Alone Again (Naturally)			3:40	Gilbert O'Sullivan
71	17	15	11	50	O ●	Joy To The World			3:17	Three Dog Night
60	16	14	11	51	O ●	Are You Lonesome To-night?			3:07	Elvis Presley
58	14	14	10	52	O	The Purple People Eater	[N]		2:11	Sheb Wooley
70	14	13	10	53	O ●	Bridge Over Troubled Water			4:55	Simon & Garfunkel
84	19	14	9	54	O ●	Like A Virgin			3:35	Madonna
69	13	12	9	55	O ●	In The Year 2525 (Exordium & Terminus)			3:15	Zager & Evans

Pos 1 5 Wks

YR	CH	40	10	RANK	GOLD	PEAK POSITION	PEAK WEEKS	SYM	TIME	ARTIST
57	31	23	16	56	O	Tammy			3:00	Debbie Reynolds
56	23	19	15	57	O	Love Me Tender			2:42	Elvis Presley
56	23	20	14	58	O	My Prayer			2:45	The Platters
80	22	19	14	59	O ●	(Just Like) Starting Over			3:54	John Lennon
77	23	17	12	60	O ●	Best Of My Love			3:40	Emotions
58	19	16	12	61	O	All I Have To Do Is Dream			2:17	The Everly Brothers
84	21	16	11	62	O ▲	When Doves Cry			3:49	Prince
60	20	16	11	63	O	It's Now Or Never			3:12	Elvis Presley
58	19	16	11	64	O	Tequila	[I]		2:09	The Champs
70	16	16	11	65	O	I'll Be There			3:35	The Jackson 5
76	19	15	11	66	O ●	Silly Love Songs			5:54	Wings
71	17	15	11	67	O ●	Maggie May			5:15	Rod Stewart
62	18	14	11	68	O ●	I Can't Stop Loving You			2:37	Ray Charles
58	20	16	10	69	O ●	Don't			2:48	Elvis Presley
84	21	15	10	70	O ●	Jump			4:04	Van Halen
79	20	15	10	71	O ▲	Bad Girls			3:55	Donna Summer
68	18	15	10	72	O ●	Love Is Blue	[I]		2:31	Paul Mauriat
71	17	15	10	73	O ●	It's Too Late			3:51	Carole King
59	17	14	10	74	O	Venus			2:21	Frankie Avalon
62	16	14	10	75	O	Big Girls Don't Cry			2:25	The 4 Seasons
58	16	13	10	76	O	Nel Blu Dipinto Di Blu (Volare)	[F]		3:29	Domenico Modugno
61	16	13	10	77	O ●	Big Bad John	[S]		2:57	Jimmy Dean
63	15	13	10	78	O ●	Sugar Shack			2:01	Jimmy Gilmer & The Fireballs
68	15	13	10	79	O ●	Honey			3:58	Bobby Goldsboro
67	17	15	9	80	O ●	To Sir With Love			2:44	Lulu
60	17	13	9	81	O	Cathy's Clown			2:22	The Everly Brothers
73	16	13	9	82	O ●	Killing Me Softly With His Song			4:46	Roberta Flack
68	14	13	9	83	O ●	People Got To Be Free			2:57	The Rascals
71	15	12	9	84	O ●	One Bad Apple			2:45	The Osmonds
69	12	12	9	85	O ●	Get Back			3:08	The Beatles with Billy Preston
66	13	11	9	86	O ●	The Ballad Of The Green Berets			2:27	SSgt Barry Sadler
62	14	12	7	87	O ●	Sherry			2:07	The 4 Seasons
64	10	9	6	88	O ●	Can't Buy Me Love			2:12	The Beatles

Pos 1 4 Wks

YR	CH	40	10	RANK	GOLD	PEAK POSITION	PEAK WEEKS	SYM	TIME	ARTIST
55	26	26	18	89	O	Autumn Leaves	[I]		2:52	Roger Williams
56	29	24	17	90	O	Lisbon Antigua	[I]		2:33	Nelson Riddle
77	31	23	16	91	O ●	I Just Want To Be Your Everything			3:32	Andy Gibb

YR	CH	40	10	RANK	G O L D	PEAK POSITION	S Y M	TIME	ARTIST

Pos 1 — 4 Wks Cont'd

YR	CH	40	10	RANK	GOLD	PEAK POSITION	TIME	ARTIST
56	23	19	14	92	O	I Almost Lost My Mind	2:27	Pat Boone
80	29	17	14	93	O ●	Upside Down	3:37	Diana Ross
57	28	23	13	94	O	Honeycomb	2:14	Jimmie Rodgers
78	27	22	13	95	O ▲	Stayin' Alive	3:29	Bee Gees
70	22	19	13	96	O ●	Raindrops Keep Fallin' On My Head	3:02	B.J. Thomas
83	24	17	13	97	O ●	All Night Long (All Night)	4:16	Lionel Richie
82	23	17	13	98	O ●	Maneater	4:30	Daryl Hall & John Oates
57	26	20	12	99	O	Wake Up Little Susie	1:57	The Everly Brothers
80	25	19	12	100	O ●	Another Brick In The Wall (Part II)	3:10	Pink Floyd
58	23	19	12	101	O	Sugartime	2:29	The McGuire Sisters
69	22	18	12	102	O ●	Sugar, Sugar	2:48	The Archies
79	21	18	12	103	O ▲	Da Ya Think I'm Sexy?	5:21	Rod Stewart
78	23	17	12	104	O ●	Kiss You All Over	3:30	Exile
80	22	17	12	105	O ●	Crazy Little Thing Called Love	2:44	Queen
83	29	18	11	106	O ●	Total Eclipse Of The Heart	4:29	Bonnie Tyler
73	23	17	11	107	O ●	Tie A Yellow Ribbon Round The Ole Oak Tree	3:19	Dawn Featuring Tony Orlando
72	19	17	11	108	O ●	American Pie - Parts I & II	8:36	Don McLean
70	17	15	11	109	O ●	(They Long To Be) Close To You	3:40	Carpenters
68	16	14	11	110	O ●	(Sittin' On) The Dock Of The Bay	2:38	Otis Redding
69	15	14	11	111	O ●	Honky Tonk Women	3:03	The Rolling Stones
83	25	19	10	112	O ●	Down Under	3:41	Men At Work
86	23	17	10	113	O ●	That's What Friends Are For	3:58	Dionne & Friends
82	22	17	10	114	O ●	Jack & Diane	4:16	John Cougar
79	23	15	10	115	O ▲	Reunited	3:58	Peaches & Herb
90	21	15	10	116	O ▲	Nothing Compares 2 U	5:09	Sinead O'Connor
59	21	15	10	117	O	Stagger Lee	2:20	Lloyd Price
89	18	14	10	118	O ●	Another Day In Paradise	4:48	Phil Collins
59	17	14	10	119	O	The Three Bells	2:47	The Browns
59	15	14	10	120	O	Lonely Boy	2:33	Paul Anka
71	15	14	10	121	O ●	How Can You Mend A Broken Heart	3:52	The Bee Gees
60	16	13	10	122	O	Stuck On You	2:17	Elvis Presley
62	15	13	10	123	O ●	Roses Are Red (My Love)	2:37	Bobby Vinton
70	14	13	10	124	O ●	My Sweet Lord	4:39	George Harrison
67	16	12	10	125	O ●	Daydream Believer	2:57	The Monkees
80	24	19	9	126	O ▲	Rock With You	3:20	Michael Jackson
80	23	16	9	127	O ●	Magic	4:25	Olivia Newton-John
85	20	16	9	128	O ●	Say You, Say Me	3:59	Lionel Richie
80	23	15	9	129	O ▲	Funkytown	3:57	Lipps, Inc.
87	20	15	9	130	O ●	Faith	3:14	George Michael
73	18	15	9	131	O ●	My Love	4:07	Paul McCartney & Wings
69	19	14	9	132	O ●	Everyday People	2:18	Sly & The Family Stone
72	19	14	9	133	O ●	Without You	3:16	Nilsson
58	19	14	9	134	O ●	He's Got The Whole World (In His Hands)	2:20	Laurie London
69	15	13	9	135	O ●	Dizzy	2:55	Tommy Roe
67	14	13	9	136	O ●	Windy	2:49	The Association
67	20	12	9	137	O ●	Ode To Billie Joe	4:13	Bobbie Gentry
61	17	12	9	138	O	Runaway	2:20	Del Shannon
63	15	12	9	139	O	He's So Fine	1:53	The Chiffons
65	14	12	9	140	O ●	(I Can't Get No) Satisfaction	3:45	The Rolling Stones
63	13	12	9	141	O	Dominique [F]	2:53	The Singing Nun
64	13	12	9	142	O	There! I've Said It Again	2:20	Bobby Vinton
67	13	11	9	143	O ●	Somethin' Stupid	2:35	Nancy Sinatra & Frank Sinatra
67	13	11	9	144	O ●	Groovin'	2:25	The Young Rascals

YR	CH	40	10	RANK	GOLD	PEAK POSITION	SYM	TIME	ARTIST

Pos 1 4 Wks Cont'd

YR	CH	40	10	RANK	GOLD	PEAK POSITION	TIME	ARTIST
86	23	15	8	145	O ●	Walk Like An Egyptian	3:21	Bangles
76	20	15	8	146	O ●	Don't Go Breaking My Heart	4:23	Elton John & Kiki Dee
72	20	14	8	147	O ●	I Can See Clearly Now	2:48	Johnny Nash
89	20	13	8	148	O ▲	Miss You Much	3:55	Janet Jackson
76	19	13	8	149	O ▲	Disco Lady	4:20	Johnnie Taylor
67	16	13	8	150	O ●	The Letter	1:58	The Box Tops
85	18	12	8	151	O ▲	We Are The World	6:22	USA for Africa
59	16	12	8	152	O	Come Softly To Me	2:25	Fleetwoods
68	14	12	8	153	O ●	This Guy's In Love With You	3:55	Herb Alpert
64	13	12	8	154	O	Baby Love	2:34	The Supremes
90	22	17	7	155	O ●	Vision Of Love	3:22	Mariah Carey
88	18	14	7	156	O	Roll With It	4:30	Steve Winwood
87	21	13	7	157	O	Livin' On A Prayer	4:12	Bon Jovi
75	23	16	6	158	O ●	Love Will Keep Us Together	3:15	The Captain & Tennille
58	28	13	6	159	O	The Chipmunk Song [X-N]	2:17	The Chipmunks/David Seville
65	11	9	6	160	O ●	Yesterday	2:04	The Beatles

Pos 1 3 Wks

YR	CH	40	10	RANK	GOLD	PEAK POSITION	TIME	ARTIST
60	39	33	25	161	O	The Twist	2:32	Chubby Checker
56	26	22	18	162	O	The Green Door	2:11	Jim Lowe
77	33	26	17	163	O ●	How Deep Is Your Love	3:30	Bee Gees
56	27	22	15	164	O	Moonglow and Theme From "Picnic" [I]	2:47	Morris Stoloff
80	31	21	15	165	O ▲	Another One Bites The Dust	3:32	Queen
79	21	17	14	166	O ▲	Hot Stuff	3:47	Donna Summer
77	25	18	13	167	O ●	Love Theme From "A Star Is Born" (Evergreen)	3:03	Barbra Streisand
79	27	17	13	168	O ▲	I Will Survive	3:15	Gloria Gaynor
57	26	17	13	169	O	You Send Me	2:41	Sam Cooke
82	28	21	12	170	O ●	Don't You Want Me	3:56	The Human League
58	19	18	12	171	O	Witch Doctor [N]	2:15	David Seville
81	24	17	12	172	O ●	Arthur's Theme (Best That You Can Do)	3:53	Christopher Cross
78	23	17	12	173	O ▲	Boogie Oogie Oogie	3:45	A Taste Of Honey
80	24	19	11	174	O ●	Woman In Love	3:48	Barbra Streisand
60	23	18	11	175	O	I'm Sorry	2:40	Brenda Lee
58	23	18	11	176	O	To Know Him, Is To Love Him	2:18	The Teddy Bears
84	23	16	11	177	O ▲	Footloose	3:46	Kenny Loggins
80	21	16	11	178	O ●	Coming Up (Live at Glasgow)	3:54	Paul McCartney & Wings
70	19	16	11	179	O ●	I Think I Love You	2:28	The Partridge Family
71	18	16	11	180	O ●	Knock Three Times	2:56	Dawn
62	18	14	11	181	O	Peppermint Twist - Part I	2:00	Joey Dee & the Starliters
73	17	14	11	182	O ●	You're So Vain	4:25	Carly Simon
84	28	18	10	183	O ●	What's Love Got To Do With It	3:49	Tina Turner
83	25	18	10	184	O ▲	Beat It	4:11	Michael Jackson
76	25	18	10	185	O ▲	Play That Funky Music	3:12	Wild Cherry
78	32	16	10	186	O ●	Baby Come Back	3:28	Player
84	24	16	10	187	O ●	Against All Odds (Take A Look At Me Now)	3:24	Phil Collins
79	21	16	10	188	O ●	Escape (The Pina Colada Song)	3:50	Rupert Holmes
59	19	16	10	189	O	Smoke Gets In Your Eyes	2:39	The Platters
84	26	15	10	190	O ●	I Just Called To Say I Love You	4:16	Stevie Wonder
61	17	15	10	191	O	Wonderland By Night [I]	3:12	Bert Kaempfert
60	27	14	10	192	O	Running Bear	2:33	Johnny Preston
84	21	14	10	193	O ●	Ghostbusters	3:46	Ray Parker Jr.
57	20	14	10	194	O	Butterfly	2:17	Andy Williams

YR	WEEKS			RANK	G O L D		PEAK POSITION	PEAK WEEKS	S Y M	TIME	ARTIST
	CH	40	10								

Pos **1** **3** Wks Cont'd

YR	CH	40	10	RANK			TITLE	SYM	TIME	ARTIST
71	18	14	10	195	O	●	Brand New Key		2:26	Melanie
66	15	13	10	196	O	●	Winchester Cathedral		2:23	The New Vaudeville Band
72	14	12	10	197	O	●	A Horse With No Name		4:10	America
74	23	17	9	198	O	●	The Way We Were		3:29	Barbra Streisand
85	21	17	9	199	O	●	Careless Whisper		4:50	Wham! Featuring George Michael
84	22	16	9	200	O	●	Karma Chameleon		4:05	Culture Club
78	20	15	9	201	O	●	MacArthur Park		3:59	Donna Summer
67	23	14	9	202	O	●	Light My Fire		2:52	The Doors
60	18	14	9	203	O		Save The Last Dance For Me		2:34	The Drifters
73	17	14	9	204	O	●	Crocodile Rock		3:56	Elton John
57	17	14	9	205	O	●	Too Much		2:30	Elvis Presley
72	18	13	9	206	O	●	Baby Don't Get Hooked On Me		3:02	Mac Davis
71	15	13	9	207	O	●	Go Away Little Girl		2:30	Donny Osmond
71	14	13	9	208	O	●	Family Affair		3:04	Sly & The Family Stone
70	14	13	9	209	O	●	Ain't No Mountain High Enough		3:15	Diana Ross
67	15	12	9	210	O	●	Happy Together		2:50	The Turtles
63	15	12	9	211	O	●	Hey Paula		2:25	Paul & Paula
63	14	12	9	212	O		My Boyfriend's Back		2:11	The Angels
81	23	17	8	213	O	●	Kiss On My List		3:48	Daryl Hall & John Oates
90	24	16	8	214	O	▲	Vogue		4:19	Madonna
74	21	15	8	215	O	●	Seasons In The Sun		3:24	Terry Jacks
87	21	15	8	216	O		Alone		3:38	Heart
90	17	15	8	217	O	●	Escapade		4:41	Janet Jackson
84	24	14	8	218	O	●	Wake Me Up Before You Go-Go		3:51	Wham!
88	21	14	8	219	O	●	Every Rose Has Its Thorn		4:20	Poison
85	18	14	8	220	O	●	Can't Fight This Feeling		4:54	REO Speedwagon
61	16	14	8	221	O		Pony Time		2:27	Chubby Checker
72	16	14	8	222	O	●	Me And Mrs. Jones		4:42	Billy Paul
64	15	14	8	223	O	●	Oh, Pretty Woman		2:55	Roy Orbison
70	15	14	8	224	O	●	American Woman		3:51	The Guess Who
69	15	14	8	225	O	●	Wedding Bell Blues		2:42	The 5th Dimension
85	22	13	8	226	O		Money For Nothing		4:38	Dire Straits
87	18	13	8	227	O		With Or Without You		4:56	U2
77	17	13	8	228	O		Sir Duke		3:53	Stevie Wonder
62	16	13	8	229	O		Telstar	[I]	3:14	The Tornadoes
70	15	13	8	230	O		War		3:12	Edwin Starr
61	15	13	8	231	O	●	The Lion Sleeps Tonight		2:35	The Tokens
62	14	13	8	232	O		Soldier Boy		2:40	The Shirelles
74	17	12	8	233	O	●	The Streak	[N]	3:15	Ray Stevens
63	15	12	8	234	O		Blue Velvet		2:46	Bobby Vinton
62	15	12	8	235	O		Hey! Baby		2:23	Bruce Channel
63	14	12	8	236	O		Sukiyaki	[F]	3:05	Kyu Sakamoto
62	15	11	8	237	O		Duke Of Earl		2:22	Gene Chandler
65	14	11	8	238	O		Turn! Turn! Turn! (To Everything There Is A Season)		3:34	The Byrds
61	14	11	8	239	O		Blue Moon		2:15	The Marcels
63	14	11	8	240	O		I Will Follow Him		2:25	Little Peggy March
66	13	11	8	241	O	●	(You're My) Soul And Inspiration		3:00	The Righteous Brothers
66	12	10	8	242	O	●	Monday, Monday		3:09	The Mama's & The Papa's
67	11	10	8	243	O	●	Hello Goodbye		3:24	The Beatles
64	11	10	8	244	O		The House Of The Rising Sun		2:58	The Animals
89	25	16	7	245	O	▲	Straight Up		4:11	Paula Abdul
72	21	16	7	246	O	●	The Candy Man		3:10	Sammy Davis, Jr.
82	23	15	7	247	O	▲	Up Where We Belong		4:00	Joe Cocker & Jennifer Warnes

YR	WEEKS			RANK	G O L D	PEAK POSITION	PEAK WEEKS	S Y M	TIME	ARTIST
	CH	40	10							

Pos 1 3 Wks Cont'd

YR	CH	40	10	RANK	GOLD	PEAK POSITION		SYM	TIME	ARTIST
86	23	15	7	248	O ●	On My Own			4:30	Patti LaBelle & Michael McDonald
90	23	14	7	249	O ●	Opposites Attract			3:45	Paula Abdul with The Wild Pair
87	21	14	7	250	O	La Bamba	[F]		2:54	Los Lobos
72	19	14	7	251	O ●	Lean On Me			3:45	Bill Withers
86	18	14	7	252	O	Greatest Love Of All			4:30	Whitney Houston
88	18	14	7	253	O ●	One More Try			5:50	George Michael
89	21	13	7	254	O ▲	Right Here Waiting			4:21	Richard Marx
85	19	13	7	255	O ●	Shout			3:59	Tears For Fears
86	19	13	7	256	O	Stuck With You			4:20	Huey Lewis & The News
75	17	13	7	257	O ●	Fly, Robin, Fly	[I]		3:05	Silver Convention
86	17	13	7	258	O	Rock Me Amadeus			3:10	Falco
89	19	12	7	259	O ●	Lost In Your Eyes			3:34	Debbie Gibson
89	16	12	7	260	O ▲	Like A Prayer			5:19	Madonna
75	15	12	7	261	O ●	Island Girl			3:46	Elton John
63	15	12	7	262	O	Fingertips - Pt 2			2:49	Little Stevie Wonder
68	13	12	7	263	O ●	Mrs. Robinson			4:00	Simon & Garfunkel
63	13	12	7	264	O	Walk Like A Man			2:11	The 4 Seasons
61	15	11	7	265	O	Take Good Care Of My Baby			2:27	Bobby Vee
90	15	11	7	266	O ▲	Step By Step			4:18	New Kids On The Block
64	13	11	7	267	O	Chapel Of Love			2:45	The Dixie Cups
66	12	11	7	268	O ●	We Can Work It Out			2:10	The Beatles
65	11	11	7	269	O ●	Mrs. Brown You've Got A Lovely Daughter			2:46	Herman's Hermits
64	11	11	7	270	O ●	I Feel Fine			2:20	The Beatles
65	14	10	7	271	O ●	I Got You Babe			3:09	Sonny & Cher
66	11	10	7	272	O ●	Summer In The City			2:39	The Lovin' Spoonful
90	23	16	6	273	O	How Am I Supposed To Live Without You			4:14	Michael Bolton
76	27	15	6	274	O ●	December, 1963 (Oh, What a Night)			3:21	The Four Seasons
76	17	13	6	275	O ●	50 Ways To Leave Your Lover			3:29	Paul Simon
66	14	12	6	276	O ●	Cherish			3:00	The Association
65	13	12	6	277	O ●	Help!			2:16	The Beatles
74	15	11	6	278	O ●	(You're) Having My Baby			2:32	Paul Anka
75	14	10	6	279	O ●	He Don't Love You (Like I Love You)			3:36	Tony Orlando & Dawn
75	14	12	5	280	O ●	Bad Blood			3:06	Neil Sedaka

Pos 1 2 Wks

YR	CH	40	10	RANK	GOLD	PEAK POSITION		SYM	TIME	ARTIST
55	21	21	18	281	O	Learnin' The Blues			2:59	Frank Sinatra
55	20	20	15	282	O	Ain't That A Shame			2:22	Pat Boone
57	29	19	14	283	O	Round And Round			2:30	Perry Como
82	25	19	14	284	O ●	Abracadabra			3:34	The Steve Miller Band
56	24	19	14	285	O	The Great Pretender			2:38	The Platters
73	19	17	13	286	O	Let's Get It On			3:58	Marvin Gaye
81	32	22	12	287	O ●	Jessie's Girl			3:14	Rick Springfield
83	25	18	12	288	O ▲	Islands In The Stream			4:08	Kenny Rogers & Dolly Parton
82	24	18	12	289	O ●	Hard To Say I'm Sorry			3:42	Chicago
78	29	22	11	290	O ●	(Love Is) Thicker Than Water			3:18	Andy Gibb
80	21	19	11	291	O ●	It's Still Rock And Roll To Me			2:55	Billy Joel
78	20	16	11	292	O	Three Times A Lady			3:35	Commodores
79	21	15	11	293	O	Ring My Bell			3:30	Anita Ward
69	17	15	11	294	O	I Can't Get Next To You			2:53	The Temptations
68	16	15	11	295	O	Love Child			2:59	Diana Ross & The Supremes
69	16	15	11	296	O	Crimson And Clover			3:23	Tommy James & The Shondells
58	15	15	11	297	O	Poor Little Fool			2:29	Ricky Nelson
79	19	14	11	298	O ●	Babe			4:26	Styx
64	15	14	11	299	O	She Loves You			2:18	The Beatles

They've done it again—
The dynamic duo...

MARVIN GAYE
&
TAMMI TERRELL

"YOU'RE ALL I NEED TO GET BY"

Tamla 54169

MOTOWN
RECORD CORPORATION
"The Sound of Young America"

YR	CH	40	10	RANK	GOLD	PEAK POSITION		TIME	ARTIST

Pos **1** **2** Wks Cont'd

70	14	13	11	300	O ●	Let It Be	3:50	The Beatles

♪ ♪ ♪ ♪ ♪ ♪

YR	CH	40	10	RANK	GOLD	Title	TIME	ARTIST
84	24	17	10	301	O ●	Hello	4:07	Lionel Richie
84	23	17	10	302	O	Owner Of A Lonely Heart	3:50	Yes
58	21	17	10	303	O	It's Only Make Believe	2:10	Conway Twitty
77	22	16	10	304	O ●	Torn Between Two Lovers	3:40	Mary MacGregor
59	20	16	10	305	O	Heartaches By The Number	2:39	Guy Mitchell
73	19	16	10	306	O	Keep On Truckin' (Part 1)	3:21	Eddie Kendricks
78	17	15	10	307	O ●	You Don't Bring Me Flowers	3:14	Barbra Streisand & Neil Diamond
60	18	14	10	308	O	Teen Angel	2:38	Mark Dinning
60	17	14	10	309	O	My Heart Has A Mind Of Its Own	2:25	Connie Francis
70	16	14	10	310	O	The Tears Of A Clown	2:56	Smokey Robinson & The Miracles
82	18	13	10	311	O ●	Truly	3:19	Lionel Richie
65	14	13	10	312	O	I Can't Help Myself	2:43	Four Tops
83	32	18	9	313	O ●	Baby, Come To Me	3:30	Patti Austin with James Ingram
81	28	18	9	314	O ●	I Love A Rainy Night	3:08	Eddie Rabbitt
81	26	18	9	315	O ●	9 To 5	2:42	Dolly Parton
75	23	18	9	316	O ●	Rhinestone Cowboy	3:08	Glen Campbell
76	26	17	9	317	O ▲	Kiss And Say Goodbye	3:29	Manhattans
90	25	17	9	318	O ●	It Must Have Been Love	3:43	Roxette
81	23	17	9	319	O ●	Private Eyes	3:29	Daryl Hall & John Oates
75	21	17	9	320	O ●	Philadelphia Freedom	5:38	The Elton John Band
76	21	17	9	321	O ●	If You Leave Me Now	3:53	Chicago
79	21	17	9	322	O ▲	Too Much Heaven	4:54	Bee Gees
84	23	16	9	323	O	Out Of Touch	3:55	Daryl Hall John Oates
83	22	16	9	324	O	Maniac	4:13	Michael Sembello
60	22	16	9	325	O	El Paso	4:40	Marty Robbins
79	25	15	9	326	O ●	Rise	[I] 3:47	Herb Alpert
85	22	15	9	327	O	Broken Wings	4:29	Mr. Mister
84	20	14	9	328	O ●	Time After Time	3:59	Cyndi Lauper
84	19	14	9	329	O ●	Let's Hear It For The Boy	4:20	Deniece Williams
84	19	14	9	330	O ●	Let's Go Crazy	3:46	Prince & The Revolution
87	18	14	9	331	O ▲	I Wanna Dance With Somebody (Who Loves Me)	4:36	Whitney Houston
71	16	14	9	332	O ●	Gypsys, Tramps & Thieves	2:36	Cher
79	20	13	9	333	O ▲	Tragedy	5:00	Bee Gees
76	18	13	9	334	O	Love Hangover	3:40	Diana Ross
59	18	13	9	335	O	Sleep Walk	[I] 2:20	Santo & Johnny
61	17	13	9	336	O ●	Calcutta	[I] 2:13	Lawrence Welk
65	16	13	9	337	O	You've Lost That Lovin' Feelin'	3:05	The Righteous Brothers
75	16	13	9	338	O ●	That's The Way (I Like It)	3:06	KC & The Sunshine Band
64	15	13	9	339	O ●	I Get Around	2:12	The Beach Boys
71	15	13	9	340	O	Just My Imagination (Running Away With Me)	3:39	The Temptations
65	15	13	9	341	O ●	Downtown	2:58	Petula Clark
62	15	13	9	342	O	Johnny Angel	2:16	Shelley Fabares
70	15	13	9	343	O ●	Mama Told Me (Not To Come)	2:58	Three Dog Night
68	15	13	9	344	O ●	Tighten Up	2:38	Archie Bell & The Drells
79	15	13	9	345	O ●	No More Tears (Enough Is Enough)	4:39	Barbra Streisand/Donna Summer
64	14	13	9	346	O	Come See About Me	2:39	The Supremes
64	14	13	9	347	O	Where Did Our Love Go	2:32	The Supremes
63	17	12	9	348	O	Go Away Little Girl	2:07	Steve Lawrence
61	14	12	9	349	O ●	Runaround Sue	2:40	Dion
70	13	12	9	350	O	ABC	2:38	The Jackson 5

YR	WEEKS			RANK	GOLD	PEAK POSITION	PEAK WEEKS	SYM	TIME	ARTIST
	CH	40	10							

Pos **1** **2** Wks Cont'd

YR	CH	40	10	RANK			TIME	ARTIST
70	13	12	9	351	O	The Love You Save	2:42	The Jackson 5
71	13	12	9	352	O	Theme From Shaft	3:15	Isaac Hayes
64	13	12	9	353	O	Do Wah Diddy Diddy	2:19	Manfred Mann
61	17	11	9	354	O	Michael	2:45	The Highwaymen
65	12	11	9	355	O ●	This Diamond Ring	2:05	Gary Lewis & The Playboys
68	12	11	9	356	O ●	Hello, I Love You	2:13	The Doors
62	37	24	8	357	O ●	Monster Mash [N]	3:01	Bobby "Boris" Pickett & The Crypt-Kickers
88	24	16	8	358	O ●	Look Away	3:59	Chicago
73	22	16	8	359	O ●	Bad, Bad Leroy Brown	3:02	Jim Croce
85	21	16	8	360	O ●	I Want To Know What Love Is	4:58	Foreigner
73	20	16	8	361	O ●	Top Of The World	2:56	Carpenters
73	19	16	8	362	O ●	Midnight Train To Georgia	3:55	Gladys Knight & The Pips
60	18	16	8	363	O	Everybody's Somebody's Fool	2:40	Connie Francis
78	22	15	8	364	O ▲	Grease	3:21	Frankie Valli
87	22	15	8	365	O ●	Nothing's Gonna Stop Us Now	4:29	Starship
84	21	15	8	366	O	The Reflex	4:25	Duran Duran
85	19	15	8	367	O ●	The Power Of Love	3:53	Huey Lewis & The News
89	19	15	8	368	O ●	We Didn't Start The Fire	4:29	Billy Joel
73	18	15	8	369	O ●	Brother Louie	3:55	Stories
61	16	15	8	370	O ●	Travelin' Man	2:12	Ricky Nelson
85	24	14	8	371	O	Everybody Wants To Rule The World	4:10	Tears For Fears
73	22	14	8	372	O ●	Will It Go Round In Circles	3:42	Billy Preston
73	20	14	8	373	O ●	Half-Breed	2:42	Cher
81	20	14	8	374	O ●	Rapture	6:33	Blondie
76	20	14	8	375	O ●	Afternoon Delight	3:12	Starland Vocal Band
57	17	14	8	376	O	Butterfly	2:21	Charlie Gracie
69	16	13	8	377	O ●	Na Na Hey Hey Kiss Him Goodbye	3:45	Steam
68	16	13	8	378	O ●	Judy In Disguise (With Glasses)	2:47	John Fred & His Playboy Band
64	15	13	8	379	O	My Guy	2:45	Mary Wells
58	15	13	8	380	O	Get A Job	2:25	The Silhouettes
78	18	12	8	381	O	With A Little Luck	5:45	Wings
74	18	12	8	382	O ●	Kung Fu Fighting	3:18	Carl Douglas
75	17	12	8	383	O ●	Jive Talkin'	3:33	Bee Gees
59	16	12	8	384	O	Kansas City	2:21	Wilbert Harrison
71	15	12	8	385	O	Me And Bobby McGee	4:09	Janis Joplin
61	15	12	8	386	O	Quarter To Three	2:29	U.S. Bonds
69	14	12	8	387	O ●	Love Theme From Romeo & Juliet [I]	2:29	Henry Mancini
64	13	12	8	388	O ●	A Hard Day's Night	2:28	The Beatles
71	12	12	8	389	O	Brown Sugar	3:50	The Rolling Stones
61	13	11	8	390	O	Hit The Road Jack	2:00	Ray Charles
66	13	11	8	391	O	You Can't Hurry Love	2:49	The Supremes
61	12	11	8	392	O	Surrender	1:51	Elvis Presley
65	12	10	8	393	O	Stop! In The Name Of Love	2:51	The Supremes
66	11	9	8	394	O	Wild Thing	2:30	The Troggs
81	30	21	7	395	O ▲	Celebration	3:42	Kool & The Gang
84	26	15	7	396	O ●	Caribbean Queen (No More Love On The Run)	3:32	Billy Ocean
85	24	15	7	397	O ●	We Built This City	4:49	Starship
90	24	15	7	398	O ●	Black Velvet	4:45	Alannah Myles
90	22	15	7	399	O ●	Release Me	3:40	Wilson Phillips
61	19	15	7	400	O	Will You Love Me Tomorrow	2:48	The Shirelles

♪   ♪   ♪   ♪   ♪   ♪

YR	CH	40	10	RANK			TIME	ARTIST
88	24	14	7	401	O ●	Never Gonna Give You Up	3:31	Rick Astley
88	24	14	7	402	O ●	Sweet Child O' Mine	5:55	Guns N' Roses

YR	WEEKS			RANK	G O L D	PEAK POSITION	PEAK WEEKS	S Y M	TIME	ARTIST
	CH	40	10							

Pos 1 2 Wks Cont'd

YR	CH	40	10	RANK	GOLD	TITLE	TIME	ARTIST
88	23	14	7	403	O ●	Anything For You	4:02	Gloria Estefan & Miami Sound Machine
85	22	14	7	404	O	St. Elmo's Fire (Man In Motion)	4:08	John Parr
73	20	14	7	405	O ●	The Night The Lights Went Out In Georgia	3:36	Vicki Lawrence
88	20	14	7	406	O	Get Outta My Dreams, Get Into My Car	4:43	Billy Ocean
90	18	14	7	407	O ●	She Ain't Worth It	3:31	Glenn Medeiros/Bobby Brown
86	20	13	7	408	O	Kyrie	4:10	Mr. Mister
86	18	13	7	409	O ●	Kiss	3:46	Prince & The Revolution
86	18	13	7	410	O	Papa Don't Preach	3:47	Madonna
89	18	13	7	411	O	Two Hearts	3:23	Phil Collins
87	17	13	7	412	O	I Still Haven't Found What I'm Looking For	4:36	U2
88	17	13	7	413	O	Man In The Mirror	4:55	Michael Jackson
87	17	13	7	414	O	Didn't We Almost Have It All	4:56	Whitney Houston
74	19	12	7	415	O ●	Billy, Don't Be A Hero	3:25	Bo Donaldson & The Heywoods
62	18	12	7	416	O	He's A Rebel	2:25	The Crystals
87	17	12	7	417	O	I Knew You Were Waiting (For Me)	3:57	Aretha Franklin & George Michael
73	15	12	7	418	O ●	Time In A Bottle	2:24	Jim Croce
66	15	12	7	419	O	Reach Out I'll Be There	2:58	Four Tops
63	15	12	7	420	O	I'm Leaving It Up To You	2:13	Dale & Grace
62	14	12	7	421	O	Breaking Up Is Hard To Do	2:20	Neil Sedaka
70	13	12	7	422	O ●	Thank You (Falettinme Be Mice Elf Agin)	4:47	Sly & The Family Stone
74	17	11	7	423	O ●	Annie's Song	2:58	John Denver
65	14	11	7	424	O	Help Me, Rhonda	2:45	The Beach Boys
62	13	11	7	425	O	Good Luck Charm	2:23	Elvis Presley
63	13	11	7	426	O	Surf City	2:24	Jan & Dean
63	13	11	7	427	O	It's My Party	2:19	Lesley Gore
63	13	11	7	428	O	Walk Right In	2:32	The Rooftop Singers
64	12	11	7	429	O ●	Rag Doll	2:31	The 4 Seasons
67	12	11	7	430	O ●	Respect	2:26	Aretha Franklin
59	14	10	7	431	O	A Big Hunk O' Love	2:12	Elvis Presley
63	13	10	7	432	O	Easier Said Than Done	2:08	The Essex
67	13	10	7	433	O	Kind Of A Drag	2:05	The Buckinghams
68	12	10	7	434	O ●	Grazing In The Grass [I]	2:25	Hugh Masekela
66	11	10	7	435	O	Paint It, Black	3:19	The Rolling Stones
73	22	17	6	436	O ●	The Most Beautiful Girl	2:42	Charlie Rich
86	23	16	6	437	O	How Will I Know	4:10	Whitney Houston
87	24	15	6	438	O ●	At This Moment	4:10	Billy Vera & The Beaters
89	22	15	6	439	O ●	When I See You Smile	4:16	Bad English
81	21	15	6	440	O ●	Morning Train (Nine To Five)	3:20	Sheena Easton
88	27	14	6	441	O	The Flame	4:30	Cheap Trick
89	23	14	6	442	O ▲	Blame It On The Rain	4:06	Milli Vanilli
89	22	14	6	443	O ●	Forever Your Girl	4:12	Paula Abdul
89	22	14	6	444	O ●	Girl I'm Gonna Miss You	4:19	Milli Vanilli
86	21	14	6	445	O ●	Glory Of Love	4:20	Peter Cetera
75	21	14	6	446	O ●	Fame	3:30	David Bowie
74	20	14	6	447	O ●	The Loco-Motion	2:45	Grand Funk
88	20	14	6	448	O	Could've Been	3:31	Tiffany
85	20	14	6	449	O	Everything She Wants	5:10	Wham!
77	20	14	6	450	O ●	Rich Girl	2:23	Daryl Hall & John Oates
85	19	14	6	451	O	Heaven	4:03	Bryan Adams
74	18	14	6	452	O ●	TSOP (The Sound Of Philadelphia) [I]	3:29	MFSB with The Three Degrees
58	16	14	6	453	O ●	Hard Headed Woman	1:52	Elvis Presley
88	26	13	6	454	O ●	Don't Worry Be Happy	3:45	Bobby McFerrin
88	25	13	6	455	O ●	Groovy Kind Of Love	3:28	Phil Collins
87	24	13	6	456	O	I Think We're Alone Now	3:47	Tiffany

YR	WEEKS			RANK	G O L D	PEAK POSITION	PEAK WEEKS	S Y M	TIME	ARTIST
	CH	40	10							

Pos **1** 2 Wks Cont'd

YR	CH	40	10	RANK	GOLD	PEAK POSITION	SYM	TIME	ARTIST
89	20	13	6	457	O ●	Toy Soldiers..		4:52	Martika
77	20	13	6	458	O ▲	Star Wars Theme/Cantina Band................ [I]		3:28	Meco
86	19	13	6	459	O	When I Think Of You.............................		3:56	Janet Jackson
87	19	13	6	460	O	(I Just) Died In Your Arms....................		4:38	Cutting Crew
88	18	13	6	461	O	Where Do Broken Hearts Go..................		4:37	Whitney Houston
85	17	13	6	462	O	A View To A Kill...................................		3:33	Duran Duran
88	17	13	6	463	O	Father Figure.......................................		5:37	George Michael
70	15	13	6	464	O ●	Everything Is Beautiful........................		3:29	Ray Stevens
88	20	12	6	465	O ●	Bad Medicine.......................................		3:52	Bon Jovi
86	20	12	6	466	O	True Colors..		3:45	Cyndi Lauper
85	18	12	6	467	O ●	One More Night....................................		4:25	Phil Collins
86	18	12	6	468	O	Amanda..		4:16	Boston
74	18	12	6	469	O ●	I Can Help..		2:57	Billy Swan
87	17	12	6	470	O ●	Lean On Me..		3:58	Club Nouveau
72	17	12	6	471	O ●	My Ding-A-Ling............................... [N]		4:18	Chuck Berry
88	16	12	6	472	O	Monkey..		4:45	George Michael
73	15	11	6	473	O ●	The Morning After................................		2:14	Maureen McGovern
62	14	11	6	474	O ●	Sheila...		2:02	Tommy Roe
63	14	11	6	475	O	If You Wanna Be Happy........................		2:14	Jimmy Soul
65	12	11	6	476	O	Get Off Of My Cloud............................		2:58	The Rolling Stones
75	14	10	6	477	O ●	Lucy In The Sky With Diamonds.............		5:58	Elton John
66	13	10	6	478	O ●	When A Man Loves A Woman.................		2:55	Percy Sledge
66	12	10	6	479	O	You Keep Me Hangin' On......................		2:45	The Supremes
66	12	10	6	480	O	Hanky Panky..		2:59	Tommy James & The Shondells
70	10	10	6	481	O	The Long And Winding Road.................		3:40	The Beatles
65	10	10	6	482	O	I Hear A Symphony..............................		2:41	The Supremes
66	13	9	6	483	O	My Love...		2:50	Petula Clark
65	11	8	6	484	O	I'm Telling You Now.............................		2:05	Freddie & The Dreamers
66	14	12	5	485	O ●	The Sounds Of Silence.........................		3:05	Simon & Garfunkel
87	14	11	5	486	O	Bad..		4:05	Michael Jackson
74	24	10	5	487	O ●	I Honestly Love You..............................		3:36	Olivia Newton-John
74	17	10	5	488	O	Rock Your Baby....................................		3:14	George McCrae
66	10	10	5	489	O ●	Paperback Writer..................................		2:25	The Beatles
65	10	9	5	490	O ●	Eight Days A Week................................		2:43	The Beatles

Pos **1** 1 Wks

YR	CH	40	10	RANK	GOLD	PEAK POSITION	SYM	TIME	ARTIST
58	21	17	15	491	O ●	Patricia... [I]		2:28	Perez Prado
80	27	22	14	492	O ●	Do That To Me One More Time..............		3:45	The Captain & Tennille
56	23	20	14	493	O ●	Hot Diggity (Dog Ziggity Boom).............		2:19	Perry Como
57	28	22	13	494	O	Chances Are..		3:00	Johnny Mathis
56	24	19	13	495	O	I Want You, I Need You, I Love You........		2:37	Elvis Presley
64	22	19	13	496	O	Hello, Dolly!..		2:22	Louis Armstrong
57	22	19	12	497	O	Don't Forbid Me...................................		2:14	Pat Boone
57	21	17	13	498	O	Young Love..		2:29	Sonny James
79	20	15	13	499	O	Still...		3:43	Commodores
57	29	18	12	500	O	Diana...		2:29	Paul Anka

♪   ♪   ♪   ♪   ♪   ♪

YR	CH	40	10	RANK	GOLD	PEAK POSITION	SYM	TIME	ARTIST
58	21	18	12	501	O ●	Tom Dooley..		3:01	The Kingston Trio
82	21	17	12	502	O ●	I Can't Go For That (No Can Do)............		3:50	Daryl Hall & John Oates
58	23	16	12	503	O ●	Catch A Falling Star..............................		2:25	Perry Como
58	17	14	12	504	O	Twilight Time.......................................		2:47	The Platters
80	26	18	11	505	O	Please Don't Go...................................		3:43	K.C. & The Sunshine Band
59	20	17	11	506	O	Mr. Blue...		2:18	The Fleetwoods
76	21	16	11	507	O	(Shake, Shake, Shake) Shake Your Booty.....		3:06	KC & The Sunshine Band

19

YR	WEEKS			RANK	G O L D	PEAK POSITION	PEAK WEEKS		S Y M	TIME	ARTIST
	CH	40	10								

Pos **1** **1** Wks Cont'd

YR	CH	40	10	RANK	GOLD		TITLE		TIME	ARTIST
58	19	16	11	508	O		Little Star		2:37	The Elegants
62	21	15	11	509	O	●	Stranger On The Shore	[I]	2:52	Mr. Acker Bilk
58	18	15	11	510	O		Bird Dog		2:12	The Everly Brothers
76	28	22	10	511	O	●	A Fifth Of Beethoven	[I]	3:02	Walter Murphy/Big Apple Band
82	27	18	10	512	O	▲	Mickey		3:36	Toni Basil
81	26	17	10	513	O	●	The Tide Is High		3:50	Blondie
76	25	16	10	514	O	▲	Disco Duck (Part 1)	[N]	3:15	Rick Dees & His Cast Of Idiots
78	22	16	10	515	O	●	If I Can't Have You		2:57	Yvonne Elliman
76	20	16	10	516	O	●	I Write The Songs		3:39	Barry Manilow
57	23	15	10	517	O		Party Doll		2:12	Buddy Knox/The Rhythm Orchids
69	17	15	10	518	O	●	Leaving On A Jet Plane		3:27	Peter, Paul & Mary
83	20	14	10	519	O	●	Let's Dance		4:08	David Bowie
75	17	14	10	520	O		One Of These Nights		3:28	Eagles
72	16	14	10	521	O	●	Brandy (You're A Fine Girl)		2:55	Looking Glass
76	16	14	10	522	O	●	Love Rollercoaster		2:52	Ohio Players
70	17	13	10	523	O	●	Make It With You		3:14	Bread
81	28	20	9	524	O	▲	Keep On Loving You		3:22	REO Speedwagon
79	24	20	9	525	O	●	Pop Muzik		3:20	M
79	27	19	9	526	O	●	Sad Eyes		3:30	Robert John
78	31	18	9	527	O	▲	Hot Child In The City		3:06	Nick Gilder
90	25	18	9	528	O	●	Hold On		3:32	Wilson Phillips
82	27	17	9	529	O		Who Can It Be Now?		3:20	Men At Work
83	26	17	9	530	O	●	Sweet Dreams (Are Made of This)		3:36	Eurythmics
78	24	16	9	531	O	▲	You're The One That I Want		2:49	John Travolta & Olivia Newton-John
84	24	16	9	532	O		Missing You		3:58	John Waite
57	22	16	9	533	O	●	That'll Be The Day		2:14	The Crickets
85	21	16	9	534	O		Separate Lives		4:06	Phil Collins & Marilyn Martin
78	20	16	9	535	O	●	Miss You		3:31	The Rolling Stones
70	19	16	9	536	O		I Want You Back		2:44	The Jackson 5
74	18	16	9	537	O	●	Bennie And The Jets		5:10	Elton John
69	16	16	9	538	O	●	Come Together		4:16	The Beatles
82	28	15	9	539	O	●	Chariots Of Fire - Titles	[I]	3:15	Vangelis
71	22	15	9	540	O	●	Indian Reservation		2:55	Raiders
77	18	15	9	541	O		Got To Give It Up (Pt. I)		3:58	Marvin Gaye
69	16	15	9	542	O		Someday We'll Be Together		3:14	Diana Ross & The Supremes
72	16	15	9	543	O	●	Let's Stay Together		3:15	Al Green
58	16	15	9	544	O		Yakety Yak		1:50	The Coasters
77	23	14	9	545	O	▲	Car Wash		3:18	Rose Royce
85	21	14	9	546	O	●	Crazy For You		4:08	Madonna
79	20	14	9	547	O	●	What A Fool Believes		3:41	The Doobie Brothers
79	19	14	9	548	O	●	Good Times		3:42	Chic
67	16	14	9	549	O	●	Incense And Peppermints		2:37	Strawberry Alarm Clock
64	15	14	9	550	O		Mr. Lonely		2:37	Bobby Vinton
62	17	13	9	551	O		The Stripper	[I]	1:57	David Rose
79	15	13	9	552	O	●	Heartache Tonight		4:26	Eagles
70	14	13	9	553	O	●	Venus		3:05	The Shocking Blue
59	16	12	9	554	O		Why		2:30	Frankie Avalon
66	15	12	9	555	O	●	96 Tears		2:38	? & The Mysterians
66	15	12	9	556	O	●	Last Train To Clarksville		2:40	The Monkees
68	13	12	9	557	O	●	Harper Valley P.T.A.		3:12	Jeannie C. Riley
77	26	18	8	558	O	●	You Don't Have To Be A Star (To Be In My Show)		3:40	Marilyn McCoo & Billy Davis, Jr.
78	26	17	8	559	O	●	You Needed Me		3:38	Anne Murray
88	25	17	8	560	O		Need You Tonight		3:01	INXS

YR	CH	40	10	RANK	GOLD	PEAK POSITION		SYM	TIME	ARTIST

Pos **1** ¹ Wks Cont'd

YR	CH	40	10	RANK	GOLD	Title	PEAK WEEKS	TIME	ARTIST
77	24	17	8	561	O	Don't Leave Me This Way		3:35	Thelma Houston
77	21	17	8	562	O ●	You Make Me Feel Like Dancing		2:48	Leo Sayer
87	22	16	8	563	O	Shake You Down		4:04	Gregory Abbott
73	21	16	8	564	O	Touch Me In The Morning		3:51	Diana Ross
74	20	16	8	565	O ●	The Joker		3:36	Steve Miller Band
85	23	15	8	566	O ●	Everytime You Go Away		4:10	Paul Young
77	22	15	8	567	O ●	Dancing Queen		3:50	Abba
86	22	15	8	568	O	The Way It Is		4:57	Bruce Hornsby & The Range
88	22	15	8	569	O	Got My Mind Set On You		3:50	George Harrison
89	21	15	8	570	O ●	Cold Hearted		3:34	Paula Abdul
75	21	15	8	571	O ●	Before The Next Teardrop Falls		2:32	Freddy Fender
77	21	15	8	572	O ●	Southern Nights		2:58	Glen Campbell
77	20	15	8	573	O ●	Blinded By The Light		3:48	Manfred Mann's Earth Band
77	19	15	8	574	O ●	Hotel California		6:08	Eagles
74	19	15	8	575	O ●	Then Came You		3:53	Dionne Warwicke & Spinners
77	17	15	8	576	O ●	I Wish		3:37	Stevie Wonder
75	23	14	8	577	O ●	My Eyes Adored You		3:25	Frankie Valli
85	22	14	8	578	O	Don't You (Forget About Me)		4:20	Simple Minds
72	22	14	8	579	O ●	I Am Woman		3:04	Helen Reddy
81	21	14	8	580	O ●	Stars on 45		4:05	Stars on 45
85	21	14	8	581	O	Part-Time Lover		3:43	Stevie Wonder
73	20	14	8	582	O ●	Delta Dawn		3:08	Helen Reddy
88	19	14	8	583	O	So Emotional		3:46	Whitney Houston
81	19	14	8	584	O ●	The One That You Love		4:07	Air Supply
90	19	14	8	585	O ▲	Blaze Of Glory		5:30	Jon Bon Jovi
72	15	14	8	586	O ●	I'll Take You There		3:19	The Staple Singers
77	20	13	8	587	O ●	Gonna Fly Now	[I]	2:45	Bill Conti
89	18	13	8	588	O ●	Don't Wanna Lose You		4:10	Gloria Estefan
75	18	13	8	589	O ●	Lovin' You		3:20	Minnie Riperton
71	16	13	8	590	O ●	Want Ads		2:34	The Honey Cone
64	15	13	8	591	O ●	Everybody Loves Somebody		2:40	Dean Martin
60	15	13	8	592	O	Itsy Bitsy Teenie Weenie Yellow Polkadot Bikini	[N]	2:19	Brian Hyland
72	14	13	8	593	O ●	Heart Of Gold		2:59	Neil Young
60	15	12	8	594	O	Alley-Oop	[N]	2:36	Hollywood Argyles
61	14	12	8	595	O	Mother-In-Law		2:25	Ernie K-Doe
71	14	12	8	596	O ●	You've Got A Friend		4:26	James Taylor
78	18	11	8	597	O ●	Too Much, Too Little, Too Late		3:00	Johnny Mathis/Deniece Williams
65	13	11	8	598	O	My Girl		2:55	The Temptations
64	12	11	8	599	O	A World Without Love		2:38	Peter & Gordon
77	25	17	7	600	O ●	Undercover Angel		3:24	Alan O'Day

♪   ♪   ♪   ♪   ♪   ♪

YR	CH	40	10	RANK	GOLD	Title	PEAK WEEKS	TIME	ARTIST
88	27	16	7	601	O ●	Wild, Wild West		3:59	The Escape Club
74	22	16	7	602	O ●	Love's Theme	[I]	3:30	Love Unlimited Orchestra
74	22	16	7	603	O ●	Show And Tell		3:28	Al Wilson
89	29	15	7	604	O ●	Wind Beneath My Wings		4:54	Bette Midler
85	27	15	7	605	O	Take On Me		3:46	a-ha
89	24	15	7	606	O ●	My Prerogative		4:25	Bobby Brown
61	23	15	7	607	O	Please Mr. Postman		2:20	The Marvelettes
85	22	15	7	608	O	Saving All My Love For You		3:48	Whitney Houston
76	21	15	7	609	O ●	Boogie Fever		3:25	Sylvers
86	20	15	7	610	O	Human		3:46	Human League
75	20	15	7	611	O	Laughter In The Rain		2:50	Neil Sedaka
83	18	15	7	612	O	Tell Her About It		3:35	Billy Joel
87	28	14	7	613	O	Here I Go Again		3:52	Whitesnake

ZOOMMING
EAST TO WEST...NORTH TO SOUTH

AIN'T TOO PROUD TO BEG

GORDY 7054

THE TEMPTATIONS

MOTOWN
RECORD CORP.
DETROIT, MICH.
The Sound of Young America

YR	WEEKS			RANK	G O L D	PEAK POSITION	PEAK WEEKS	S Y M	TIME	ARTIST
	CH	40	10							

Pos **1** **1** Wks Cont'd

YR	CH	40	10	RANK	GOLD	PEAK POSITION	SYM	TIME	ARTIST
89	23	14	7	614	O ●	She Drives Me Crazy		3:35	Fine Young Cannibals
86	22	14	7	615	O ●	Addicted To Love		3:59	Robert Palmer
87	22	14	7	616	O	Always		3:59	Atlantic Starr
79	21	14	7	617	O ●	Heart Of Glass		3:22	Blondie
86	21	14	7	618	O	There'll Be Sad Songs (To Make You Cry)		4:02	Billy Ocean
86	21	14	7	619	O	Sledgehammer		4:58	Peter Gabriel
86	20	14	7	620	O	West End Girls		3:55	Pet Shop Boys
77	20	14	7	621	O ●	When I Need You		4:11	Leo Sayer
87	20	14	7	622	O	Head To Toe		3:58	Lisa Lisa & Cult Jam
73	20	14	7	623	O ●	Frankenstein	[I]	3:28	The Edgar Winter Group
74	19	14	7	624	O ●	You Haven't Done Nothin		3:20	Stevie Wonder
87	18	14	7	625	O	Shakedown		3:59	Bob Seger
74	18	14	7	626	O ●	Nothing From Nothing		2:40	Billy Preston
75	18	14	7	627	O ●	(Hey Won't You Play) Another Somebody Done Somebody Wrong Song		3:23	B.J. Thomas
59	17	14	7	628	O	The Happy Organ	[I]	2:01	Dave 'Baby' Cortez
74	17	14	7	629	O ●	Hooked On A Feeling		2:54	Blue Swede
70	15	14	7	630	O ●	Cracklin' Rosie		2:47	Neil Diamond
72	15	14	7	631	O	Oh Girl		3:16	Chi-Lites
85	22	13	7	632	O	Miami Vice Theme	[I]	2:26	Jan Hammer
86	21	13	7	633	O	Take My Breath Away		4:13	Berlin
80	21	13	7	634	O	Sailing		4:15	Christopher Cross
90	20	13	7	635	O	If Wishes Came True		5:09	Sweet Sensation
86	20	13	7	636	O	Sara		4:18	Starship
77	19	13	7	637	O ●	Don't Give Up On Us		3:30	David Soul
89	19	13	7	638	O ●	The Look		3:56	Roxette
77	19	13	7	639	O ●	Dreams		4:14	Fleetwood Mac
74	18	13	7	640	O ●	Sunshine On My Shoulders		3:18	John Denver
74	18	13	7	641	O ●	Band On The Run		5:09	Paul McCartney & Wings
75	18	13	7	642	O	Lady Marmalade		3:14	LaBelle
73	17	13	7	643	O	You Are The Sunshine Of My Life		2:45	Stevie Wonder
75	17	13	7	644	O ●	Pick Up The Pieces	[I]	3:00	AWB (Average White Band)
76	17	13	7	645	O	Theme From Mahogany (Do You Know Where You're Going To)		3:19	Diana Ross
73	16	13	7	646	O ●	Angie		4:30	The Rolling Stones
77	15	13	7	647	O ●	New Kid In Town		4:49	Eagles
77	22	12	7	648	O ●	Da Doo Ron Ron		2:46	Shaun Cassidy
76	20	12	7	649	O ●	You Should Be Dancing		4:15	Bee Gees
86	19	12	7	650	O	Venus		3:49	Bananarama
76	19	12	7	651	O	Let Your Love Flow		3:16	Bellamy Brothers
75	19	12	7	652	O ●	The Hustle	[I]	3:27	Van McCoy
75	17	12	7	653	O ●	Black Water		4:17	The Doobie Brothers
62	16	12	7	654	O	The Loco-Motion		2:12	Little Eva
61	16	12	7	655	O	Wooden Heart		2:00	Joe Dowell
74	15	12	7	656	O ●	You're Sixteen		2:50	Ringo Starr
75	15	12	7	657	O ●	Let's Do It Again		3:28	The Staple Singers
66	15	12	7	658	O	Poor Side Of Town		3:03	Johnny Rivers
63	15	12	7	659	O	So Much In Love		3:08	The Tymes
63	15	12	7	660	O	Deep Purple		2:41	Nino Tempo & April Stevens
66	14	12	7	661	O ●	These Boots Are Made For Walkin'		2:40	Nancy Sinatra
66	14	12	7	662	O ●	Good Vibrations		3:35	The Beach Boys
66	14	12	7	663	O	Good Lovin'		2:28	The Young Rascals
71	13	12	7	664	O ●	Uncle Albert/Admiral Halsey		4:47	Paul & Linda McCartney
68	13	12	7	665	O ●	Green Tambourine		2:22	The Lemon Pipers
74	18	11	7	666	O ●	Sundown		3:37	Gordon Lightfoot

YR	WEEKS			RANK	GOLD	PEAK POSITION	PEAK WEEKS	SYM	TIME	ARTIST
	CH	40	10							

Pos 1 1 Wks Cont'd

YR	CH	40	10	RANK	GOLD	PEAK POSITION		TIME	ARTIST
72	16	11	7	667	O	Ben		2:42	Michael Jackson
75	16	11	7	668	O ●	Have You Never Been Mellow		3:28	Olivia Newton-John
76	16	11	7	669	O ●	Convoy	[N]	3:48	C.W. McCall
66	15	11	7	670	O	Strangers In The Night		2:35	Frank Sinatra
75	14	11	7	671	O ●	Listen To What The Man Said		3:53	Wings
76	14	11	7	672	O ●	Welcome Back		2:48	John Sebastian
73	14	11	7	673	O	Give Me Love - (Give Me Peace On Earth)		3:32	George Harrison
65	14	11	7	674	O	Hang On Sloopy		2:57	The McCoys
60	13	10	7	675	O	Mr. Custer	[N]	2:59	Larry Verne
66	13	10	7	676	O	Sunshine Superman		3:11	Donovan
65	13	10	7	677	O	Mr. Tambourine Man		2:18	The Byrds
64	12	10	7	678	O	Ringo	[S]	3:00	Lorne Greene
67	11	10	7	679	O	Love Is Here And Now You're Gone		2:35	The Supremes
65	11	10	7	680	O	Eve Of Destruction		3:28	Barry McGuire
67	12	9	7	681	O ●	Ruby Tuesday		3:12	The Rolling Stones
67	11	9	7	682	O ●	All You Need Is Love		3:57	The Beatles
76	28	19	6	683	O ●	Love Machine (Part 1)		2:55	The Miracles
88	40	16	6	684	O ●	Red Red Wine		5:21	UB40
77	23	16	6	685	O	I'm Your Boogie Man		3:58	KC & The Sunshine Band
83	21	16	6	686	O	Africa		4:23	Toto
88	20	16	6	687	O	Seasons Change		3:58	Expose
88	25	15	6	688	O	Wishing Well		3:33	Terence Trent D'Arby
88	24	15	6	689	O ●	Baby, I Love Your Way/Freebird Medley (Free Baby)		4:07	Will To Power
89	22	15	6	690	O ●	If You Don't Know Me By Now		3:24	Simply Red
87	21	15	6	691	O	Heaven Is A Place On Earth		3:49	Belinda Carlisle
87	21	15	6	692	O ●	(I've Had) The Time Of My Life		4:47	Bill Medley & Jennifer Warnes
86	21	15	6	693	O	The Next Time I Fall		3:43	Peter Cetera w/Amy Grant
90	20	15	6	694	O ●	Love Will Lead You Back		4:18	Taylor Dayne
86	24	14	6	695	O	You Give Love A Bad Name		3:53	Bon Jovi
83	23	14	6	696	O	Come On Eileen		4:12	Dexys Midnight Runners
86	23	14	6	697	O	Holding Back The Years		4:04	Simply Red
86	22	14	6	698	O	Higher Love		4:08	Steve Winwood
89	22	14	6	699	O	Listen To Your Heart		5:26	Roxette
89	21	14	6	700	O ●	I'll Be Loving You (Forever)		3:54	New Kids On The Block
88	21	14	6	701	O	Hold On To The Nights		4:34	Richard Marx
89	21	14	6	702	O ●	Baby Don't Forget My Number		4:01	Milli Vanilli
79	20	14	6	703	O ▲	Knock On Wood		3:40	Amii Stewart
89	20	14	6	704	O	The Living Years		5:30	Mike & The Mechanics
88	20	14	6	705	O	Foolish Beat		4:20	Debbie Gibson
75	19	14	6	706	O	Best Of My Love		3:25	The Eagles
89	19	14	6	707	O ●	Eternal Flame		3:56	Bangles
87	18	14	6	708	O	Open Your Heart		4:12	Madonna
85	17	14	6	709	O ●	Sussudio		4:23	Phil Collins
88	23	13	6	710	O	Love Bites		5:46	Def Leppard
89	22	13	6	711	O	I'll Be There For You		5:43	Bon Jovi
85	21	13	6	712	O	Oh Sheila		3:36	Ready For The World
87	21	13	6	713	O	You Keep Me Hangin' On		4:13	Kim Wilde
86	20	13	6	714	O	These Dreams		3:46	Heart
87	20	13	6	715	O	Lost In Emotion		3:59	Lisa Lisa & Cult Jam
74	18	13	6	716	O ●	Rock Me Gently		3:28	Andy Kim
86	18	13	6	717	O	Live To Tell		4:37	Madonna
88	18	13	6	718	O	The Way You Make Me Feel		4:26	Michael Jackson
74	17	13	6	719	O ●	Angie Baby		3:29	Helen Reddy

YR	WEEKS			RANK	GOLD	PEAK POSITION	PEAK WEEKS	SYM	TIME	ARTIST
	CH	40	10							

Pos 1 1 Wks Cont'd

YR	CH	40	10	RANK	GOLD	TITLE	PEAK	TIME	ARTIST
73	17	13	6	720	O ●	We're An American Band		3:25	Grand Funk
89	17	13	6	721	O	Good Thing		3:22	Fine Young Cannibals
73	16	13	6	722	O	Superstition		3:59	Stevie Wonder
74	16	13	6	723	O ●	Feel Like Makin' Love		2:55	Roberta Flack
60	15	13	6	724	O	I Want To Be Wanted		3:00	Brenda Lee
69	15	13	6	725	O ●	Suspicious Minds		4:22	Elvis Presley
73	14	13	6	726	O ●	Love Train		2:59	O'Jays
76	24	12	6	727	O ●	Theme From S.W.A.T.	[I]	2:47	Rhythm Heritage
87	22	12	6	728	O	Mony Mony "Live"		4:00	Billy Idol
79	21	12	6	729	O ▲	Don't Stop 'Til You Get Enough		5:45	Michael Jackson
74	19	12	6	730	O ●	Cat's In The Cradle		3:29	Harry Chapin
88	18	12	6	731	O	Together Forever		3:20	Rick Astley
76	17	12	6	732	O ●	Saturday Night		2:56	Bay City Rollers
86	17	12	6	733	O	Invisible Touch		3:26	Genesis
75	17	12	6	734	O ●	Fallin' In Love		3:13	Hamilton, Joe Frank & Reynolds
89	17	12	6	735	O ▲	Hangin' Tough		3:51	New Kids On The Block
73	16	12	6	736	O ●	Photograph		3:59	Ringo Starr
74	16	12	6	737	O ●	Dark Lady		3:26	Cher
72	16	12	6	738	O	Papa Was A Rollin' Stone		6:58	The Temptations
61	15	12	6	739	O	Moody River		2:38	Pat Boone
87	15	12	6	740	O	Jacob's Ladder		3:28	Huey Lewis & The News
72	13	12	6	741	O ●	Song Sung Blue		3:15	Neil Diamond
89	18	11	6	742	O ▲	Batdance		4:06	Prince
74	17	11	6	743	O ●	The Night Chicago Died		3:30	Paper Lace
87	16	11	6	744	O	Who's That Girl		3:58	Madonna
64	14	11	6	745	O	Love Me Do		2:18	The Beatles
87	14	11	6	746	O ●	I Just Can't Stop Loving You		4:17	Michael Jackson/Siedah Garrett
65	12	11	6	747	O	Over And Over		2:00	The Dave Clark Five
66	15	10	6	748	O ●	Lightnin' Strikes		2:44	Lou Christie
63	13	10	6	749	O	Our Day Will Come		2:31	Ruby & The Romantics
62	13	10	6	750	O	Don't Break The Heart That Loves You		2:58	Connie Francis
67	11	10	6	751	O	The Happening		2:50	The Supremes
65	11	9	6	752	O	Ticket To Ride		3:02	The Beatles
65	10	8	6	753	O ●	I'm Henry VIII, I Am		1:49	Herman's Hermits
88	28	15	5	754	O ▲	Kokomo		3:34	The Beach Boys
75	19	15	5	755	O ●	Thank God I'm A Country Boy		2:47	John Denver
75	20	14	5	756	O ●	Shining Star		2:50	Earth, Wind & Fire
76	18	14	5	757	O	Rock'n Me		3:05	Steve Miller
60	18	14	5	758	O	Stay		1:50	Maurice Williams & The Zodiacs
89	28	13	5	759	O ●	When I'm With You		3:54	Sheriff
89	21	13	5	760	O ●	Rock On		3:21	Michael Damian
77	19	13	5	761	O ●	Looks Like We Made It		3:29	Barry Manilow
79	19	13	5	762	O ●	Love You Inside Out		3:48	Bee Gees
90	18	13	5	763	O ●	I'll Be Your Everything		3:58	Tommy Page
89	15	13	5	764	O	Satisfied		3:58	Richard Marx
74	17	12	5	765	O ●	You Ain't Seen Nothing Yet		3:29	Bachman-Turner Overdrive
75	17	12	5	766	O ●	Please Mr. Postman		2:48	Carpenters
75	16	12	5	767	O ●	Mandy		3:15	Barry Manilow
88	14	11	5	768	O	Dirty Diana		4:37	Michael Jackson
74	18	10	5	769	O ●	Rock The Boat		3:03	The Hues Corporation
75	16	10	5	770	O	You're No Good		3:40	Linda Ronstadt
74	14	10	5	771	O ●	I Shot The Sheriff		3:30	Eric Clapton
60	13	10	5	772	O	Georgia On My Mind		3:37	Ray Charles
64	12	10	5	773	O	Leader Of The Pack		2:48	The Shangri-Las

YR	WEEKS			RANK	GOLD	PEAK POSITION	PEAK WEEKS	SYM	TIME	ARTIST
	CH	40	10							

Pos 1 1 Wks Cont'd

65	11	10	5	774	O	Game Of Love			2:04	Wayne Fontana/The Mindbenders
65	11	10	5	775	O	Back In My Arms Again			2:50	The Supremes
72	11	9	5	776	O ●	Black & White			3:24	Three Dog Night
67	10	9	5	777	O ●	Penny Lane			3:00	The Beatles
61	17	15	4	778	O	Running Scared			2:10	Roy Orbison
75	18	13	4	779	O ●	I'm Sorry			3:29	John Denver
75	17	12	4	780	O ●	Fire			3:12	Ohio Players
75	16	12	4	781	O	Sister Golden Hair			3:16	America
75	15	9	4	782	O	Get Down Tonight			3:06	K.C. & The Sunshine Band
74	12	9	4	783	O ●	Can't Get Enough Of Your Love, Babe			3:15	Barry White
74	15	11	3	784	O	Whatever Gets You Thru The Night			3:20	John Lennon/Plastic Ono Band

Pos 2 10 Wks

| 81 | 23 | 19 | 15 | 785 | O ● | Waiting For A Girl Like You | | | 4:35 | Foreigner |

Pos 2 8 Wks

| 57 | 26 | 21 | 10 | 786 | O | Little Darlin' | | | 2:05 | The Diamonds |

Pos 2 6 Wks

55	25	25	19	787	O	Moments To Remember			3:14	The Four Lads
82	18	14	10	788	O	Open Arms			3:21	Journey
78	20	15	9	789	O ●	Baker Street			4:08	Gerry Rafferty
63	18	13	9	790	O	Louie Louie			2:24	The Kingsmen

Pos 2 5 Wks

82	23	18	11	791	O	Rosanna			3:59	Toto
62	16	14	10	792	O ●	Return To Sender			2:05	Elvis Presley
80	23	15	9	793	O ●	More Than I Can Say			3:40	Leo Sayer
83	22	15	8	794	O ▲	Electric Avenue			3:47	Eddy Grant

Pos 2 4 Wks

57	38	26	18	795	O	So Rare			2:30	Jimmy Dorsey
82	28	22	16	796	O ●	Hurts So Good			3:35	John Cougar
57	27	22	15	797	O	Bye Bye Love			2:17	The Everly Brothers
56	24	19	12	798	O	No, Not Much!			3:12	The Four Lads
56	21	17	11	799	O	Blue Suede Shoes			2:14	Carl Perkins
82	21	16	11	800	O	Don't Talk To Strangers			3:00	Rick Springfield

♪   ♪   ♪   ♪   ♪   ♪

80	27	17	10	801	O ●	All Out Of Love			3:41	Air Supply
60	20	15	10	802	O	Last Date	[I]		2:20	Floyd Cramer
83	18	15	10	803	O	Say It Isn't So			3:56	Daryl Hall - John Oates
80	21	17	9	804	O	Ride Like The Wind			3:54	Christopher Cross
84	21	15	9	805	O	Dancing In The Dark			3:59	Bruce Springsteen
60	20	15	9	806	O	Greenfields			3:00	The Brothers Four
70	17	14	9	807	O ●	We've Only Just Begun			3:09	Carpenters
58	21	15	8	808	O	Great Balls Of Fire			1:50	Jerry Lee Lewis
83	21	19	8	809	O	Shame On The Moon			4:55	Bob Seger/The Silver Bullet Band
84	18	14	8	810	O	The Wild Boys			4:14	Duran Duran
66	12	11	8	811	O ●	Snoopy Vs. The Red Baron	[N]		2:43	The Royal Guardsmen
64	26	16	7	812	O	Twist And Shout			2:33	The Beatles
63	15	12	7	813	O	Can't Get Used To Losing You			2:19	Andy Williams
68	13	11	7	814	O	(Theme From) Valley Of The Dolls			3:35	Dionne Warwick

YR	WEEKS			RANK	G O L D	PEAK POSITION	PEAK WEEKS	S Y M	TIME	ARTIST
	CH	40	10							

Pos 2 4 Wks Cont'd

YR	CH	40	10	RANK	G	Title		SYM	TIME	ARTIST
87	19	14	6	815	O	Looking For A New Love			3:58	Jody Watley
73	14	11	6	816	O ●	Dueling Banjos	[I]		3:17	Eric Weissberg & Steve Mandell
75	10	7	5	817	O	Calypso			3:32	John Denver

Pos 2 3 Wks

YR	CH	40	10	RANK	G	Title		SYM	TIME	ARTIST
56	39	22	16	818	O	Honky Tonk (Parts 1 & 2)	[I]		5:35	Bill Doggett
57	27	21	16	819	O	Blueberry Hill			2:14	Fats Domino
56	27	22	15	820	O	Whatever Will Be, Will Be (Que Sera, Sera)			2:01	Doris Day
55	18	17	14	821	O	I Hear You Knocking			2:20	Gale Storm
79	26	20	12	822	O ▲	Y.M.C.A.			3:30	Village People
60	23	20	12	823	O	He'll Have To Go			2:16	Jim Reeves
81	20	17	12	824	O ●	Woman			3:30	John Lennon
81	24	19	11	825	O	Start Me Up			3:32	The Rolling Stones
81	24	16	11	826	O ●	Slow Hand			3:57	Pointer Sisters
81	24	16	11	827	O	Just The Two Of Us			3:40	Grover Washington, Jr. with Bill Withers
59	18	14	11	828	O	Put Your Head On My Shoulder			2:39	Paul Anka
82	36	22	10	829	O ●	Gloria			4:50	Laura Branigan
77	26	18	10	830	O ●	Don't It Make My Brown Eyes Blue			2:37	Crystal Gayle
81	20	17	10	831	O	Love On The Rocks			3:41	Neil Diamond
81	25	16	10	832	O ●	Being With You			3:58	Smokey Robinson
59	19	14	10	833	O	Personality			2:35	Lloyd Price
83	18	14	10	834	O ●	The Girl Is Mine			3:41	Michael Jackson/Paul McCartney
83	25	18	9	835	O	Do You Really Want To Hurt Me			4:23	Culture Club
83	25	17	9	836	O ●	Making Love Out Of Nothing At All			4:29	Air Supply
76	21	17	9	837	O ●	The Rubberband Man			3:30	Spinners
76	21	15	9	838	O ●	Get Up And Boogie (That's Right)			4:05	Silver Convention
82	19	15	9	839	O ●	We Got The Beat			2:30	Go-Go's
85	22	14	9	840	O ●	Party All The Time			3:58	Eddie Murphy
67	17	14	9	841	O	I Heard It Through The Grapevine			2:52	Gladys Knight & The Pips
69	15	12	9	842	O	Crystal Blue Persuasion			3:45	Tommy James & The Shondells
77	25	15	8	843	O ●	Nobody Does It Better			3:30	Carly Simon
76	20	14	8	844	O ●	Dream Weaver			3:15	Gary Wright
58	20	14	8	845	O	26 Miles (Santa Catalina)			2:31	The Four Preps
84	19	14	8	846	O ●	Somebody's Watching Me			3:57	Rockwell
58	18	14	8	847	O	Stood Up			1:57	Ricky Nelson
68	15	13	8	848	O ●	Young Girl			3:12	Union Gap feat. Gary Puckett
71	15	13	8	849	O	What's Going On			3:40	Marvin Gaye
61	16	12	8	850	O	The Boll Weevil Song	[N]		2:35	Brook Benton
59	15	12	8	851	O	Charlie Brown	[N]		2:12	The Coasters
67	15	11	8	852	O ●	Soul Man			2:36	Sam & Dave
85	25	15	7	853	O ●	Cherish			3:58	Kool & The Gang
77	20	14	7	854	O	Keep It Comin' Love			3:48	KC & The Sunshine Band
73	17	14	7	855	O ●	Goodbye Yellow Brick Road			3:13	Elton John
68	14	12	7	856	O ●	Those Were The Days			5:05	Mary Hopkin
69	14	12	7	857	O ●	Proud Mary			3:07	Creedence Clearwater Revival
73	14	12	7	858	O ●	Live And Let Die			3:10	Wings
69	13	12	7	859	O	Spinning Wheel			2:39	Blood, Sweat & Tears
58	16	11	7	860	O	Sweet Little Sixteen			2:35	Chuck Berry
69	12	11	7	861	O ●	A Boy Named Sue	[N]		3:40	Johnny Cash
71	12	11	7	862	O	Never Can Say Goodbye			2:56	The Jackson 5
61	17	10	7	863	O	I Like It Like That, Part 1			1:55	Chris Kenner
66	12	10	7	864	O	Mellow Yellow			3:40	Donovan
90	21	14	6	865	O ●	Don't Wanna Fall In Love			4:04	Jane Child

YR	CH	40	10	RANK	GOLD	PEAK POSITION		TIME	ARTIST

Pos **2** ³ Wks Cont'd

YR	CH	40	10	RANK	GOLD	TITLE		TIME	ARTIST
76	19	14	6	866	O ●	All By Myself		4:22	Eric Carmen
89	20	13	6	867	O ▲	On Our Own		4:30	Bobby Brown
77	20	13	6	868	O	I'm In You		3:57	Peter Frampton
88	19	13	6	869	O	Shattered Dreams		3:30	Johnny Hates Jazz
86	16	12	6	870	O	Typical Male		4:14	Tina Turner
68	14	12	6	871	O ●	The Horse	[I]	2:25	Cliff Nobles & Co.
68	13	12	6	872	O ●	Born To Be Wild		2:55	Steppenwolf
81	16	11	6	873	O	All Those Years Ago		3:42	George Harrison
65	15	11	6	874	O ●	A Lover's Concerto		2:36	The Toys
63	13	11	6	875	O	Ruby Baby		2:31	Dion
69	13	11	6	876	O ●	You've Made Me So Very Happy		3:26	Blood, Sweat & Tears
63	13	10	6	877	O	Be My Baby		2:20	The Ronettes
66	10	9	6	878	O	19th Nervous Breakdown		3:50	The Rolling Stones
67	10	9	6	879	O	Dedicated To The One I Love		2:56	The Mamas & The Papas
63	10	8	6	880	O	Hello Mudduh, Hello Fadduh! (A Letter From Camp)	[C]	2:47	Allan Sherman
78	20	13	5	881	O ●	Short People	[N]	2:54	Randy Newman
87	18	11	5	882	O	Causing A Commotion		4:00	Madonna
75	17	11	5	883	O	I'm Not In Love		3:40	10cc
64	13	10	5	884	O	You Don't Own Me		2:26	Lesley Gore

Pos **2** ² Wks

YR	CH	40	10	RANK	GOLD	TITLE		TIME	ARTIST
56	31	23	14	885	O	Canadian Sunset	[I]	2:50	Hugo Winterhalter/Eddie Heywood
56	27	22	12	886	O	Allegheny Moon		2:48	Patti Page
62	23	17	12	887	O	Limbo Rock		2:22	Chubby Checker
81	27	19	10	888	O ●	Queen Of Hearts		3:29	Juice Newton
58	21	19	10	889	O	Rock-in Robin		2:25	Bobby Day
81	26	18	10	890	O ●	Theme From "Greatest American Hero" (Believe It or Not)		3:11	Joey Scarbury
59	23	18	10	891	O	Donna		2:20	Ritchie Valens
76	24	17	10	892	O ●	I'd Really Love To See You Tonight		2:36	England Dan & John Ford Coley
72	21	16	10	893	O ●	I Gotcha		2:18	Joe Tex
70	19	15	10	894	O ●	One Less Bell To Answer		3:29	The 5th Dimension
57	19	14	10	895	O	Love Me		2:39	Elvis Presley
77	27	17	9	896	O ▲	Boogie Nights		3:36	Heatwave
90	24	16	9	897	O ▲	Pump Up The Jam		3:36	Technotronic Featuring Felly
74	22	16	9	898	O	Dancing Machine		2:29	The Jackson 5
62	18	15	9	899	O	Mashed Potato Time		2:27	Dee Dee Sharp
79	21	14	9	900	O ●	Dim All The Lights		3:55	Donna Summer

♪   ♪   ♪   ♪   ♪   ♪

YR	CH	40	10	RANK	GOLD	TITLE		TIME	ARTIST
65	18	14	9	901	O ●	Wooly Bully		2:20	Sam The Sham & The Pharoahs
61	16	14	9	902	O	Bristol Stomp		2:18	The Dovells
83	18	13	9	903	O	Time (Clock Of The Heart)		3:41	Culture Club
79	17	13	9	904	O ●	After The Love Has Gone		3:55	Earth, Wind & Fire
67	16	13	9	905	O ●	Little Bit O' Soul		2:18	The Music Explosion
89	26	16	8	906	O ●	Don't Know Much		3:33	Linda Ronstadt feat. Aaron Neville
80	25	16	8	907	O ●	Working My Way Back To You/Forgive Me, Girl		4:01	Spinners
79	23	16	8	908	O ●	Fire		3:41	Pointer Sisters
73	23	15	8	909	O ●	Playground In My Mind		2:55	Clint Holmes
76	20	15	8	910	O ●	Right Back Where We Started From		3:16	Maxine Nightingale
84	25	14	8	911	O ▲	Girls Just Want To Have Fun		3:55	Cyndi Lauper
74	25	14	8	912	O ●	You Make Me Feel Brand New		4:45	The Stylistics
59	21	14	8	913	O	16 Candles		2:49	The Crests

YR	CH	40	10	RANK	GOLD	PEAK POSITION	SYM	TIME	ARTIST

Pos 2 — 2 Wks Cont'd

YR	CH	40	10	RANK	GOLD	TITLE	TIME	ARTIST
78	20	14	8	914	O ●	The Closer I Get To You	4:39	Roberta Flack with Donny Hathaway
86	17	14	8	915	O	Dancing On The Ceiling	4:20	Lionel Richie
76	21	13	8	916	O ●	You'll Never Find Another Love Like Mine	3:36	Lou Rawls
90	20	13	8	917	O ●	All I Wanna Do Is Make Love To You	4:24	Heart
60	16	13	8	918	O	Chain Gang	2:32	Sam Cooke
71	16	13	8	919	O	Mr. Big Stuff	2:27	Jean Knight
62	16	13	8	920	O	Ramblin' Rose	2:45	Nat King Cole
69	15	13	8	921	O ●	Hair	3:28	The Cowsills
72	15	13	8	922	O ●	Long Cool Woman (In A Black Dress)	3:02	The Hollies
67	16	12	8	923	O ●	The Rain, The Park & Other Things	2:57	The Cowsills
67	16	12	8	924	O ●	Georgy Girl	2:20	The Seekers
71	13	12	8	925	O ●	Superstar	3:49	Carpenters
69	13	12	8	926	O	I'm Gonna Make You Love Me	2:56	Supremes & Temptations
72	14	11	8	927	O ●	Too Late To Turn Back Now	3:12	Cornelius Brothers & Sister Rose
67	14	11	8	928	O ●	Never My Love	2:49	The Association
68	14	11	8	929	O	For Once In My Life	2:49	Stevie Wonder
72	13	11	8	930	O	Rockin' Robin	2:30	Michael Jackson
76	27	18	7	931	O	Love Is Alive	3:24	Gary Wright
85	23	16	7	932	O ●	Easy Lover	4:40	Philip Bailey/Phil Collins
80	23	16	7	933	O ●	Yes, I'm Ready	3:05	Teri DeSario with K.C.
87	23	16	7	934	O	C'est La Vie	3:28	Robbie Nevil
86	21	15	7	935	O	Everybody Have Fun Tonight	3:59	Wang Chung
86	21	14	7	936	O	Friends And Lovers	3:50	Gloria Loring & Carl Anderson
89	19	14	7	937	O ●	Heaven	3:58	Warrant
76	18	14	7	938	O ●	Love To Love You Baby	4:57	Donna Summer
74	18	14	7	939	O ●	Do It ('Til You're Satisfied)	3:09	B.T. Express
59	18	14	7	940	O	My Happiness	2:28	Connie Francis
72	18	14	7	941	O ●	Nights In White Satin	4:20	The Moody Blues
72	16	14	7	942	O ●	Clair	3:00	Gilbert O'Sullivan
80	22	13	7	943	O	Longer	3:14	Dan Fogelberg
85	21	13	7	944	O	You Belong To The City	5:51	Glenn Frey
75	19	13	7	945	O	When Will I Be Loved	2:52	Linda Ronstadt
69	16	13	7	946	O	Hot Fun In The Summertime	2:37	Sly & The Family Stone
67	15	12	7	947	O	I Was Made To Love Her	2:37	Stevie Wonder
75	15	12	7	948	O ●	You're The First, The Last, My Everything	3:25	Barry White
58	15	12	7	949	O	Lollipop	2:06	The Chordettes
69	14	12	7	950	O ●	Jean	3:11	Oliver
79	19	11	7	951	O ●	We Are Family	3:35	Sister Sledge
59	18	11	7	952	O	Sorry (I Ran All the Way Home)	2:33	The Impalas
84	16	11	7	953	O ●	Purple Rain	4:02	Prince & The Revolution
64	14	11	7	954	O	Dancing In The Street	2:37	Martha & The Vandellas
60	14	11	7	955	O	Puppy Love	2:39	Paul Anka
73	14	11	7	956	O	Kodachrome	3:29	Paul Simon
66	14	11	7	957	O ●	Lil' Red Riding Hood	2:40	Sam The Sham & The Pharoahs
71	12	11	7	958	O ●	Rainy Days And Mondays	3:40	Carpenters
64	12	11	7	959	O	Bread And Butter	1:58	The Newbeats
68	12	11	7	960	O ●	Chain Of Fools	2:45	Aretha Franklin
66	12	10	7	961	O	Daydream	2:18	The Lovin' Spoonful
67	11	10	7	962	O	Reflections	2:50	Diana Ross & The Supremes
88	29	16	6	963	O	Hands To Heaven	4:17	Breathe
86	22	16	6	964	O	Burning Heart	3:51	Survivor
88	21	15	6	965	O	Endless Summer Nights	4:11	Richard Marx
77	20	15	6	966	O ●	Fly Like An Eagle	3:00	Steve Miller
90	23	14	6	967	O ●	Two To Make It Right	4:13	Seduction

YR	CH	40	10	RANK	GOLD	PEAK POSITION		SYM	TIME	ARTIST

Pos **2** **2** Wks Cont'd

YR	CH	40	10	RANK	GOLD	TITLE	TIME	ARTIST
88	20	14	6	968	O	Simply Irresistible	4:14	Robert Palmer
59	18	14	6	969	O	Sea Of Love	2:30	Phil Phillips
76	21	13	6	970	O	The Wreck Of The Edmund Fitzgerald	5:57	Gordon Lightfoot
74	18	13	6	971	O	Boogie Down	3:30	Eddie Kendricks
85	22	12	6	972	O	All I Need	3:29	Jack Wagner
78	20	12	6	973	O ●	Double Vision	3:29	Foreigner
89	18	12	6	974	O ●	Real Love	4:19	Jody Watley
85	17	12	6	975	O	Material Girl	2:56	Madonna
90	17	12	6	976	O ●	Rhythm Nation	4:27	Janet Jackson
57	17	12	6	977	O	Teen-Age Crush	2:21	Tommy Sands
73	16	12	6	978	O	Neither One Of Us (Wants To Be The First To Say Goodbye)	4:15	Gladys Knight & The Pips
68	15	12	6	979	O ●	Cry Like A Baby	2:35	The Box Tops
73	15	12	6	980	O ●	The Cisco Kid	4:35	War
65	15	11	6	981	O	Can't You Hear My Heartbeat	2:15	Herman's Hermits
66	15	11	6	982	O ●	Sunny	2:45	Bobby Hebb
62	14	11	6	983	O	The Wah Watusi	2:30	The Orlons
68	14	11	6	984	O	Classical Gas	[I] 3:00	Mason Williams
75	14	11	6	985	O	Lyin' Eyes	3:58	The Eagles
68	13	11	6	986	O ●	Lady Willpower	2:38	Gary Puckett & The Union Gap
71	12	11	6	987	O ●	Spanish Harlem	3:30	Aretha Franklin
72	12	11	6	988	O ●	Hurting Each Other	2:46	Carpenters
69	13	10	6	989	O ●	Love (Can Make You Happy)	3:19	Mercy
64	12	10	6	990	O	Memphis	2:28	Johnny Rivers
63	12	9	6	991	O	Sally, Go 'Round The Roses	2:38	The Jaynetts
66	11	9	6	992	O	Did You Ever Have To Make Up Your Mind?	2:00	The Lovin' Spoonful
90	21	14	5	993	O	Dangerous	3:51	Roxette
88	18	13	5	994	O	What Have I Done To Deserve This?	4:19	Pet Shop Boys/Dusty Springfield
61	17	13	5	995	O	Apache	[I] 3:00	Jorgen Ingmann & His Guitar
70	17	13	5	996	O ●	Which Way You Goin' Billy?	3:10	The Poppy Family/Susan Jacks
88	17	12	5	997	O	Devil Inside	5:11	INXS
89	15	12	5	998	O	Cherish	4:03	Madonna
88	18	11	5	999	O	Mercedes Boy	3:54	Pebbles
90	17	11	5	1000	O	Come Back To Me	4:36	Janet Jackson

**Cut Yourself in
On this Philadelphia
Breakout**

Apples, Peaches, Pumpkin Pie
Jay And The Techniques

S-2086

PRODUCER: JERRY ROSS
PUBLISHED BY: PHILSTOX MUSIC PUB. INC. &
ACT THREE MUSIC (BMI)

THANKS TO DAVE CHACKLER, SMASH PROMOTION MAN IN PHILADELPHIA

If It's a Hit...It's on
⊛SMASH
RECORDS

THE YEARS

This section lists, in rank order, the Top 40 hits year-by-year. The ranking is based on the *Top 1000* ranking system.

You will note, in order to round out the Top 40 records of each year, several hundred additional hits are listed which do not appear in the *Top 1000*.

Columnar headings show the following data:

PK DATE: Date record reached its peak position
PK WKS: Total weeks record held its peak position
PK POS: Highest charted position record attained
RANK: Top 40 ranking

TOP 40 HITS
1955

PK DATE	PK WKS	PK POS	RANK	TITLE	ARTIST
7/09	8	1	1.	**Rock Around The Clock**	Bill Haley & His Comets
11/26	8	1	2.	**Sixteen Tons**	"Tennessee" Ernie Ford
10/08	6	1	3.	**Love Is A Many-Splendored Thing**	Four Aces
9/03	6	1	4.	**The Yellow Rose Of Texas**	Mitch Miller
10/29	4	1	5.	**Autumn Leaves**	Roger Williams
7/09	2	1	6.	**Learnin' The Blues**	Frank Sinatra
9/17	2	1	7.	**Ain't That A Shame**	Pat Boone
10/29	6	2	8.	**Moments To Remember**	The Four Lads
12/10	3	2	9.	**I Hear You Knocking**	Gale Storm
7/09	1	2	10.	**A Blossom Fell**	Nat "King" Cole
11/26	2	3	11.	**The Shifting, Whispering Sands**	Rusty Draper
10/08	1	3	12.	**Seventeen**	The Fontane Sisters
9/17	1	3	13.	**The Yellow Rose Of Texas**	Johnny Desmond
8/13	1	4	14.	**Hard To Get**	Gisele MacKenzie
12/31	1	4	15.	**He**	Al Hibbler
10/22	4	5	16.	**The Shifting Whispering Sands (Parts 1 & 2)**	Billy Vaughn
11/05	3	5	17.	**Only You (And You Alone)**	The Platters
11/26	3	5	18.	**Love And Marriage**	Frank Sinatra
10/15	1	5	19.	**Tina Marie**	Perry Como
7/23	1	5	20.	**Something's Gotta Give**	The McGuire Sisters
9/10	1	5	21.	**Maybellene**	Chuck Berry
9/24	1	5	22.	**Wake The Town And Tell The People**	Les Baxter
9/03	1	5	23.	**Seventeen**	Boyd Bennett & his Rockets
9/17	1	6	24.	**The Longest Walk**	Jaye P. Morgan
10/29	1	6	25.	**Black Denim Trousers**	The Cheers
11/05	1	6	26.	**You Are My Love**	Joni James
12/31	1	6	27.	**Nuttin' For Christmas**	Barry Gordon with Art Mooney
11/19	2	7	28.	**At My Front Door (Crazy Little Mama)**	Pat Boone
10/22	2	7	29.	**The Bible Tells Me So**	Don Cornell
8/27	2	7	30.	**Hummingbird**	Les Paul & Mary Ford
8/13	1	7	31.	**It's A Sin To Tell A Lie**	Somethin' Smith & The Redheads
12/31	1	7	32.	**White Christmas**	Bing Crosby
12/31	1	8	33.	**Only You (And You Alone)**	The Hilltoppers
7/16	1	8	34.	**If I May**	Nat "King" Cole & The Four Knights
7/16	1	9	35.	**Something's Gotta Give**	Sammy Davis, Jr.
8/27	1	9	36.	**The House Of Blue Lights**	Chuck Miller
12/17	1	9	37.	**Cry Me A River**	Julie London
12/31	1	9	38.	**Burn That Candle**	Bill Haley & His Comets
10/29	1	9	39.	**Suddenly There's A Valley**	Gogi Grant
7/09	3	10	40.	**Sweet And Gentle**	Alan Dale

Note The above ranking begins with the nation's first #1 rock hit "Rock Around The Clock" from the summer of 1955, and does not include the earlier hits from 1955.

TOP 40 HITS
1956

PK DATE	PK WKS	PK POS	RANK	TITLE	ARTIST
8/18	11	1	1.	Don't Be Cruel/Hound Dog	Elvis Presley
12/08	10	1	2.	Singing The Blues	Guy Mitchell
6/16	8	1	3.	The Wayward Wind	Gogi Grant
4/21	8	1	4.	Heartbreak Hotel	Elvis Presley
2/18	6	1	5.	Rock And Roll Waltz	Kay Starr
3/17	6	1	6.	The Poor People Of Paris	Les Baxter
1/07	6	1	7.	Memories Are Made Of This	Dean Martin
11/03	5	1	8.	Love Me Tender	Elvis Presley
8/04	5	1	9.	My Prayer	The Platters
2/25	4	1	10.	Lisbon Antigua	Nelson Riddle
7/28	4	1	11.	I Almost Lost My Mind	Pat Boone
11/03	3	1	12.	The Green Door	Jim Lowe
6/02	3	1	13.	Moonglow and Theme From "Picnic"	Morris Stoloff
2/18	2	1	14.	The Great Pretender	The Platters
5/05	1	1	15.	Hot Diggity (Dog Ziggity Boom)	Perry Como
7/28	1	1	16.	I Want You, I Need You, I Love You	Elvis Presley
3/17	4	2	17.	No, Not Much!	The Four Lads
5/19	4	2	18.	Blue Suede Shoes	Carl Perkins
10/06	3	2	19.	Honky Tonk (Parts 1 & 2)	Bill Doggett
8/18	3	2	20.	Whatever Will Be, Will Be (Que Sera, Sera)	Doris Day
10/13	2	2	21.	Canadian Sunset	Hugo Winterhalter/Eddie Heywood
8/18	2	2	22.	Allegheny Moon	Patti Page
10/27	1	2	23.	Just Walking In The Rain	Johnnie Ray
6/16	1	2	24.	Ivory Tower	Cathy Carr
6/16	3	3	25.	Standing On The Corner	The Four Lads
7/14	2	3	26.	I'm In Love Again	Fats Domino
11/10	1	3	27.	True Love	Bing Crosby & Grace Kelly
8/25	1	3	28.	The Flying Saucer (Parts 1 & 2)	Buchanan & Goodman
7/07	4	4	29.	On The Street Where You Live	Vic Damone
5/19	3	4	30.	(You've Got) The Magic Touch	The Platters
4/07	1	4	31.	I'll Be Home	Pat Boone
1/07	1	4	32.	Band Of Gold	Don Cherry
10/06	1	4	33.	Tonight You Belong To Me	Patience & Prudence
6/02	1	4	34.	Moonglow And Theme From "Picnic"	George Cates
7/21	1	4	35.	More	Perry Como
5/12	2	5	36.	A Tear Fell	Teresa Brewer
7/14	2	5	37.	Born To Be With You	The Chordettes
10/20	1	5	38.	Friendly Persuasion (Thee I Love)	Pat Boone
1/14	1	5	39.	Memories Are Made Of This	Gale Storm
2/11	4	6	40.	See You Later, Alligator	Bill Haley & His Comets

TOP 40 HITS
1957

PK DATE	PK WKS	PK POS	RANK	TITLE	ARTIST
4/13	9	1	1.	All Shook Up	Elvis Presley
6/03	7	1	2.	Love Letters In The Sand	Pat Boone
10/21	7	1	3.	Jailhouse Rock	Elvis Presley
7/08	7	1	4.	(Let Me Be Your) Teddy Bear	Elvis Presley
12/16	6	1	5.	April Love	Pat Boone
2/16	6	1	6.	Young Love	Tab Hunter
8/19	5	1	7.	Tammy	Debbie Reynolds
9/23	4	1	8.	Honeycomb	Jimmie Rodgers
10/14	4	1	9.	Wake Up Little Susie	The Everly Brothers
12/02	3	1	10.	You Send Me	Sam Cooke
3/30	3	1	11.	Butterfly	Andy Williams
2/09	3	1	12.	Too Much	Elvis Presley
4/06	2	1	13.	Round And Round	Perry Como
4/13	2	1	14.	Butterfly	Charlie Gracie
10/21	1	1	15.	Chances Are	Johnny Mathis
2/09	1	1	16.	Don't Forbid Me	Pat Boone
2/09	1	1	17.	Young Love	Sonny James
9/09	1	1	18.	Diana	Paul Anka
3/30	1	1	19.	Party Doll	Buddy Knox/The Rhythm Orchids
9/23	1	1	20.	That'll Be The Day	The Crickets
4/06	8	2	21.	Little Darlin'	The Diamonds
6/17	4	2	22.	So Rare	Jimmy Dorsey
6/17	4	2	23.	Bye Bye Love	The Everly Brothers
1/19	3	2	24.	Blueberry Hill	Fats Domino
1/05	2	2	25.	Love Me	Elvis Presley
3/16	2	2	26.	Teen-Age Crush	Tommy Sands
6/03	1	2	27.	A White Sport Coat (And A Pink Carnation)	Marty Robbins
12/16	1	2	28.	Raunchy	Bill Justis
6/10	1	2	29.	A Teenager's Romance	Ricky Nelson
8/05	4	3	30.	I'm Gonna Sit Right Down And Write Myself A Letter	Billy Williams
12/16	3	3	31.	Kisses Sweeter Than Wine	Jimmie Rodgers
12/30	3	3	32.	Peggy Sue	Buddy Holly
5/13	3	3	33.	School Day	Chuck Berry
9/09	2	3	34.	Whole Lot Of Shakin' Going On	Jerry Lee Lewis
11/04	2	3	35.	Silhouettes	The Rays
7/29	1	3	36.	Searchin'	The Coasters
7/29	1	3	37.	Old Cape Cod	Patti Page
1/19	1	3	38.	Moonlight Gambler	Frankie Laine
1/12	1	3	39.	Hey! Jealous Lover	Frank Sinatra
4/06	1	3	40.	Marianne	The Hilltoppers

TOP 40 HITS
1958

PK DATE	PK WKS	PK POS	RANK	TITLE	ARTIST
1/06	7	1	1.	At The Hop	Danny & The Juniors
9/29	6	1	2.	It's All In The Game	Tommy Edwards
6/09	6	1	3.	The Purple People Eater	Sheb Wooley
5/12	5	1	4.	All I Have To Do Is Dream	The Everly Brothers
3/17	5	1	5.	Tequila	The Champs
2/10	5	1	6.	Don't	Elvis Presley
8/18	5	1	7.	Nel Blu Dipinto Di Blu (Volare)	Domenico Modugno
2/17	4	1	8.	Sugartime	The McGuire Sisters
4/14	4	1	9.	He's Got The Whole World (In His Hands)	Laurie London
12/22	4	1	10.	The Chipmunk Song	The Chipmunks/David Seville
4/28	3	1	11.	Witch Doctor	David Seville
12/01	3	1	12.	To Know Him, Is To Love Him	The Teddy Bears
8/04	2	1	13.	Poor Little Fool	Ricky Nelson
11/10	2	1	14.	It's Only Make Believe	Conway Twitty
2/24	2	1	15.	Get A Job	The Silhouettes
7/21	2	1	16.	Hard Headed Woman	Elvis Presley
7/28	1	1	17.	Patricia	Perez Prado
11/17	1	1	18.	Tom Dooley	The Kingston Trio
3/24	1	1	19.	Catch A Falling Star	Perry Como
4/21	1	1	20.	Twilight Time	The Platters
8/25	1	1	21.	Little Star	The Elegants
8/25	1	1	22.	Bird Dog	The Everly Brothers
7/21	1	1	23.	Yakety Yak	The Coasters
1/06	4	2	24.	Great Balls Of Fire	Jerry Lee Lewis
3/10	3	2	25.	26 Miles (Santa Catalina)	The Four Preps
1/13	3	2	26.	Stood Up	Ricky Nelson
3/17	3	2	27.	Sweet Little Sixteen	Chuck Berry
10/13	2	2	28.	Rock-in Robin	Bobby Day
3/31	2	2	29.	Lollipop	The Chordettes
1/06	1	2	30.	All The Way	Frank Sinatra
4/28	1	2	31.	Wear My Ring Around Your Neck	Elvis Presley
12/15	1	2	32.	Problems	The Everly Brothers
6/16	3	3	33.	Secretly	Jimmie Rodgers
10/20	3	3	34.	Topsy II	Cozy Cole
6/09	2	3	35.	Big Man	The Four Preps
2/10	2	3	36.	Short Shorts	Royal Teens
8/18	1	3	37.	My True Love	Jack Scott
3/24	1	3	38.	Are You Sincere	Andy Williams
8/04	1	3	39.	Splish Splash	Bobby Darin
3/10	5	4	40.	A Wonderful Time Up There	Pat Boone

TOP 40 HITS
1959

PK DATE	PK WKS	PK POS	RANK	TITLE	ARTIST
10/05	9	1	1.	Mack The Knife	Bobby Darin
6/01	6	1	2.	The Battle Of New Orleans	Johnny Horton
3/09	5	1	3.	Venus	Frankie Avalon
2/09	4	1	4.	Stagger Lee	Lloyd Price
8/24	4	1	5.	The Three Bells	The Browns
7/13	4	1	6.	Lonely Boy	Paul Anka
4/13	4	1	7.	Come Softly To Me	Fleetwoods
1/19	3	1	8.	Smoke Gets In Your Eyes	The Platters
12/14	2	1	9.	Heartaches By The Number	Guy Mitchell
9/21	2	1	10.	Sleep Walk	Santo & Johnny
5/18	2	1	11.	Kansas City	Wilbert Harrison
8/10	2	1	12.	A Big Hunk O' Love	Elvis Presley
11/16	1	1	13.	Mr. Blue	The Fleetwoods
12/28	1	1	14.	Why	Frankie Avalon
5/11	1	1	15.	The Happy Organ	Dave 'Baby' Cortez
10/05	3	2	16.	Put Your Head On My Shoulder	Paul Anka
6/15	3	2	17.	Personality	Lloyd Price
3/09	3	2	18.	Charlie Brown	The Coasters
2/23	2	2	19.	Donna	Ritchie Valens
2/09	2	2	20.	16 Candles	The Crests
1/19	2	2	21.	My Happiness	Connie Francis
5/11	2	2	22.	Sorry (I Ran All the Way Home)	The Impalas
8/24	2	2	23.	Sea Of Love	Phil Phillips
6/08	1	2	24.	Dream Lover	Bobby Darin
11/30	1	2	25.	Don't You Know	Della Reese
8/17	1	2	26.	There Goes My Baby	The Drifters
2/02	1	2	27.	The All American Boy	Bill Parsons (Bobby Bare)
4/27	1	2	28.	(Now And Then There's) A Fool Such As I	Elvis Presley
8/03	3	3	29.	My Heart Is An Open Book	Carl Dobkins, Jr.
4/13	2	3	30.	Pink Shoe Laces	Dodie Stevens
12/28	2	3	31.	The Big Hurt	Miss Toni Fisher
9/14	2	3	32.	I'm Gonna Get Married	Lloyd Price
7/20	2	3	33.	Tiger	Fabian
3/16	2	3	34.	Alvin's Harmonica	The Chipmunks
4/06	1	3	35.	It's Just A Matter Of Time	Brook Benton
8/24	1	3	36.	Lavender-Blue	Sammy Turner
9/21	3	4	37.	('Til) I Kissed You	The Everly Brothers
7/13	3	4	38.	Waterloo	Stonewall Jackson
10/19	2	4	39.	Teen Beat	Sandy Nelson
6/01	2	4	40.	Quiet Village	Martin Denny

TOP 40 HITS
1960

PK DATE	PK WKS	PK POS	RANK	TITLE	ARTIST
2/22	9	1	1.	The Theme From "A Summer Place"	Percy Faith
11/28	6	1	2.	Are You Lonesome To-night?	Elvis Presley
8/15	5	1	3.	It's Now Or Never..................................	Elvis Presley
5/23	5	1	4.	Cathy's Clown	The Everly Brothers
4/25	4	1	5.	Stuck On You......................................	Elvis Presley
7/18	3	1	6.	I'm Sorry	Brenda Lee
1/18	3	1	7.	Running Bear	Johnny Preston
10/17	3	1	8.	Save The Last Dance For Me....................	The Drifters
2/08	2	1	9.	Teen Angel.......................................	Mark Dinning
9/26	2	1	10.	My Heart Has A Mind Of Its Own	Connie Francis
1/04	2	1	11.	El Paso..	Marty Robbins
6/27	2	1	12.	Everybody's Somebody's Fool	Connie Francis
9/19	1	1	13.	The Twist .... re-entered at #1 in 1962	Chubby Checker
8/08	1	1	14.	Itsy Bitsy Teenie Weenie Yellow Polkadot Bikini	Brian Hyland
7/11	1	1	15.	Alley-Oop..	Hollywood Argyles
10/10	1	1	16.	Mr. Custer...	Larry Verne
10/24	1	1	17.	I Want To Be Wanted	Brenda Lee
11/21	1	1	18.	Stay	Maurice Williams & The Zodiacs
11/14	1	1	19.	Georgia On My Mind..............................	Ray Charles
11/28	4	2	20.	Last Date..	Floyd Cramer
4/18	4	2	21.	Greenfields..	The Brothers Four
3/07	3	2	22.	He'll Have To Go	Jim Reeves
10/03	2	2	23.	Chain Gang..	Sam Cooke
4/04	2	2	24.	Puppy Love	Paul Anka
2/29	1	2	25.	Handy Man...	Jimmy Jones
8/29	1	2	26.	Walk—Don't Run..................................	The Ventures
7/25	1	2	27.	Only The Lonely (Know How I Feel)	Roy Orbison
3/28	1	2	28.	Wild One	Bobby Rydell
11/14	1	2	29.	Poetry In Motion	Johnny Tillotson
5/23	3	3	30.	Good Timin'.......................................	Jimmy Jones
6/13	2	3	31.	Burning Bridges...................................	Jack Scott
12/12	1	3	32.	A Thousand Stars.................................	Kathy Young with The Innocents
5/02	1	3	33.	Sixteen Reasons	Connie Stevens
4/25	1	3	34.	Sink The Bismarck	Johnny Horton
1/11	1	3	35.	Way Down Yonder In New Orleans.............	Freddie Cannon
2/08	1	3	36.	Where Or When...................................	Dion & The Belmonts
11/14	1	3	37.	You Talk Too Much	Joe Jones
5/09	2	4	38.	Night	Jackie Wilson
5/30	2	4	39.	He'll Have To Stay	Jeanne Black
7/04	2	4	40.	Because They're Young...........................	Duane Eddy & The Rebels

TOP 40 HITS
1961

PK DATE	PK WKS	PK POS	RANK	TITLE	ARTIST
7/10	7	1	1.	Tossin' And Turnin'	Bobby Lewis
11/06	5	1	2.	Big Bad John	Jimmy Dean
4/24	4	1	3.	Runaway	Del Shannon
1/09	3	1	4.	Wonderland By Night	Bert Kaempfert
2/27	3	1	5.	Pony Time	Chubby Checker
12/18	3	1	6.	The Lion Sleeps Tonight	The Tokens
4/03	3	1	7.	Blue Moon	The Marcels
9/18	3	1	8.	Take Good Care Of My Baby	Bobby Vee
2/13	2	1	9.	Calcutta	Lawrence Welk
10/23	2	1	10.	Runaround Sue	Dion
9/04	2	1	11.	Michael	The Highwaymen
5/29	2	1	12.	Travelin' Man	Ricky Nelson
6/26	2	1	13.	Quarter To Three	U.S. Bonds
10/09	2	1	14.	Hit The Road Jack	Ray Charles
3/20	2	1	15.	Surrender	Elvis Presley
1/30	2	1	16.	Will You Love Me Tomorrow	The Shirelles
5/22	1	1	17.	Mother-In-Law	Ernie K-Doe
12/11	1	1	18.	Please Mr. Postman	The Marvelettes
8/28	1	1	19.	Wooden Heart	Joe Dowell
6/19	1	1	20.	Moody River	Pat Boone
6/05	1	1	21.	Running Scared	Roy Orbison
7/10	3	2	22.	The Boll Weevil Song	Brook Benton
7/31	3	2	23.	I Like It Like That, Part 1	Chris Kenner
10/23	2	2	24.	Bristol Stomp	The Dovells
4/03	2	2	25.	Apache	Jorgen Ingmann & His Guitar
9/25	2	2	26.	The Mountain's High	Dick & DeeDee
1/23	1	2	27.	Exodus	Ferrante & Teicher
6/26	1	2	28.	Raindrops	Dee Clark
2/20	1	2	29.	Shop Around	The Miracles
12/25	1	2	30.	Run To Him	Bobby Vee
10/09	1	2	31.	Crying	Roy Orbison
5/29	1	2	32.	Daddy's Home	Shep & The Limelites
3/27	2	3	33.	Dedicated To The One I Love	The Shirelles
5/08	2	3	34.	A Hundred Pounds Of Clay	Gene McDaniels
12/04	2	3	35.	Goodbye Cruel World	James Darren
3/06	2	3	36.	Wheels	The String-A-Longs
8/07	2	3	37.	Last Night	Mar-Keys
11/13	2	3	38.	Fool #1	Brenda Lee
9/11	2	3	39.	My True Story	The Jive Five
3/20	1	3	40.	Don't Worry	Marty Robbins

TOP 40 HITS
1962

PK DATE	PK WKS	PK POS	RANK	TITLE	ARTIST
6/02	5	1	1.	I Can't Stop Loving You	Ray Charles
11/17	5	1	2.	Big Girls Don't Cry	The 4 Seasons
9/15	5	1	3.	Sherry	The 4 Seasons
7/14	4	1	4.	Roses Are Red (My Love)	Bobby Vinton
1/27	3	1	5.	Peppermint Twist - Part I	Joey Dee & the Starliters
12/22	3	1	6.	Telstar	The Tornadoes
5/05	3	1	7.	Soldier Boy	The Shirelles
3/10	3	1	8.	Hey! Baby	Bruce Channel
2/17	3	1	9.	Duke Of Earl	Gene Chandler
1/13	2	1	10.	The Twist re-entry of 1960 hit (POS 1)	Chubby Checker
4/07	2	1	11.	Johnny Angel	Shelley Fabares
11/03	2	1	12.	He's A Rebel	The Crystals
8/11	2	1	13.	Breaking Up Is Hard To Do	Neil Sedaka
10/20	2	1	14.	Monster Mash	Bobby "Boris" Pickett & The Crypt-Kickers
4/21	2	1	15.	Good Luck Charm	Elvis Presley
9/01	2	1	16.	Sheila	Tommy Roe
5/26	1	1	17.	Stranger On The Shore	Mr. Acker Bilk
7/07	1	1	18.	The Stripper	David Rose
8/25	1	1	19.	The Loco-Motion	Little Eva
3/31	1	1	20.	Don't Break The Heart That Loves You	Connie Francis
11/17	5	2	21.	Return To Sender	Elvis Presley
12/22	2	2	22.	Limbo Rock	Chubby Checker
5/05	2	2	23.	Mashed Potato Time	Dee Dee Sharp
9/22	2	2	24.	Ramblin' Rose	Nat King Cole
7/21	2	2	25.	The Wah Watusi	The Orlons
2/03	1	2	26.	Can't Help Falling In Love	Elvis Presley
2/24	1	2	27.	The Wanderer	Dion
3/17	1	2	28.	Midnight In Moscow	Kenny Ball & his Jazzmen
9/08	1	2	29.	You Don't Know Me	Ray Charles
11/03	1	2	30.	Only Love Can Break A Heart	Gene Pitney
12/01	4	3	31.	Bobby's Girl	Marcie Blane
10/20	3	3	32.	Do You Love Me	The Contours
11/10	2	3	33.	All Alone Am I	Brenda Lee
6/23	2	3	34.	Palisades Park	Freddy Cannon
7/28	2	3	35.	Sealed With A Kiss	Brian Hyland
4/14	1	3	36.	Slow Twistin'	Chubby Checker
2/24	1	3	37.	Norman	Sue Thompson
9/29	1	3	38.	Green Onions	Booker T. & The MG's
6/16	1	3	39.	It Keeps Right On A-Hurtin'	Johnny Tillotson
1/27	1	3	40.	I Know (You Don't Love Me No More)	Barbara George

TOP 40 HITS
1963

PK DATE	PK WKS	PK POS	RANK	TITLE	ARTIST
10/12	5	1	1.	Sugar Shack	Jimmy Gilmer & The Fireballs
3/30	4	1	2.	He's So Fine	The Chiffons
12/07	4	1	3.	Dominique	The Singing Nun
2/09	3	1	4.	Hey Paula	Paul & Paula
8/31	3	1	5.	My Boyfriend's Back	The Angels
9/21	3	1	6.	Blue Velvet	Bobby Vinton
6/15	3	1	7.	Sukiyaki	Kyu Sakamoto
4/27	3	1	8.	I Will Follow Him	Little Peggy March
8/10	3	1	9.	Fingertips - Pt 2	Little Stevie Wonder
3/02	3	1	10.	Walk Like A Man	The 4 Seasons
1/12	2	1	11.	Go Away Little Girl	Steve Lawrence
11/23	2	1	12.	I'm Leaving It Up To You	Dale & Grace
7/20	2	1	13.	Surf City	Jan & Dean
6/01	2	1	14.	It's My Party	Lesley Gore
1/26	2	1	15.	Walk Right In	The Rooftop Singers
7/06	2	1	16.	Easier Said Than Done	The Essex
5/18	2	1	17.	If You Wanna Be Happy	Jimmy Soul
8/03	1	1	18.	So Much In Love	The Tymes
11/16	1	1	19.	Deep Purple	Nino Tempo & April Stevens
3/23	1	1	20.	Our Day Will Come	Ruby & The Romantics
12/14	6	2	21.	Louie Louie	The Kingsmen
4/13	4	2	22.	Can't Get Used To Losing You	Andy Williams
2/23	3	2	23.	Ruby Baby	Dion
10/12	3	2	24.	Be My Baby	The Ronettes
8/24	3	2	25.	Hello Mudduh, Hello Fadduh! (A Letter From Camp)	Allan Sherman
9/28	2	2	26.	Sally, Go 'Round The Roses	The Jaynetts
8/17	1	2	27.	Blowin' In The Wind	Peter, Paul & Mary
11/23	1	2	28.	Washington Square	The Village Stompers
8/10	1	2	29.	Wipe Out	The Surfaris
3/23	1	2	30.	The End Of The World	Skeeter Davis
5/11	1	2	31.	Puff The Magic Dragon	Peter, Paul & Mary
9/07	3	3	32.	If I Had A Hammer	Trini Lopez
3/16	2	3	33.	You're The Reason I'm Living	Bobby Darin
2/02	2	3	34.	The Night Has A Thousand Eyes	Bobby Vee
12/07	2	3	35.	Everybody	Tommy Roe
8/10	2	3	36.	(You're the) Devil In Disguise	Elvis Presley
6/22	2	3	37.	Hello Stranger	Barbara Lewis
3/09	1	3	38.	Rhythm Of The Rain	The Cascades
5/25	1	3	39.	Surfin' U.S.A.	Beach Boys
6/01	1	3	40.	I Love You Because	Al Martino

TOP 40 HITS
1964

PK DATE	PK WKS	PK POS	RANK	TITLE	ARTIST
2/01	7	1	1.	I Want To Hold Your Hand	The Beatles
4/04	5	1	2.	Can't Buy Me Love	The Beatles
1/04	4	1	3.	There! I've Said It Again	Bobby Vinton
10/31	4	1	4.	Baby Love	The Supremes
9/26	3	1	5.	Oh, Pretty Woman	Roy Orbison
9/05	3	1	6.	The House Of The Rising Sun	The Animals
6/06	3	1	7.	Chapel Of Love	The Dixie Cups
12/26	3	1	8.	I Feel Fine	The Beatles
3/21	2	1	9.	She Loves You	The Beatles
7/04	2	1	10.	I Get Around	The Beach Boys
12/19	2	1	11.	Come See About Me	The Supremes
8/22	2	1	12.	Where Did Our Love Go	The Supremes
10/17	2	1	13.	Do Wah Diddy Diddy	Manfred Mann
5/16	2	1	14.	My Guy	Mary Wells
8/01	2	1	15.	A Hard Day's Night	The Beatles
7/18	2	1	16.	Rag Doll	The 4 Seasons
5/09	1	1	17.	Hello, Dolly!	Louis Armstrong
12/12	1	1	18.	Mr. Lonely	Bobby Vinton
8/15	1	1	19.	Everybody Loves Somebody	Dean Martin
6/27	1	1	20.	A World Without Love	Peter & Gordon
12/05	1	1	21.	Ringo	Lorne Greene
5/30	1	1	22.	Love Me Do	The Beatles
11/28	1	1	23.	Leader Of The Pack	The Shangri-Las
4/04	4	2	24.	Twist And Shout	The Beatles
2/01	3	2	25.	You Don't Own Me	Lesley Gore
10/17	2	2	26.	Dancing In The Street	Martha & The Vandellas
9/19	2	2	27.	Bread And Butter	The Newbeats
7/11	2	2	28.	Memphis	Johnny Rivers
11/07	1	2	29.	Last Kiss	J. Frank Wilson & The Cavaliers
12/12	1	2	30.	She's Not There	The Zombies
7/04	1	2	31.	My Boy Lollipop	Millie Small
5/09	1	2	32.	Do You Want To Know A Secret	The Beatles
2/22	3	3	33.	Dawn (Go Away)	The Four Seasons
4/11	2	3	34.	Suspicion	Terry Stafford
3/14	2	3	35.	Please Please Me	The Beatles
1/11	2	3	36.	Popsicles And Icicles	The Murmaids
2/01	2	3	37.	Out Of Limits	The Marketts
11/21	2	3	38.	Come A Little Bit Closer	Jay & The Americans
6/13	1	3	39.	Love Me With All Your Heart (Cuando Calienta El Sol)	The Ray Charles Singers
8/01	1	3	40.	The Little Old Lady (From Pasadena)	Jan & Dean

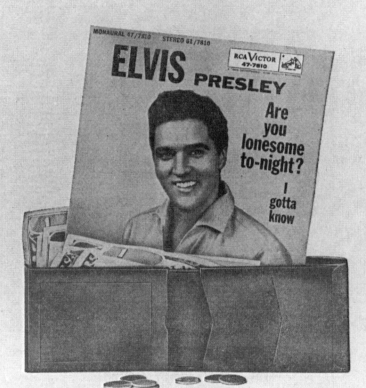

TOP 40 HITS
1965

PK DATE	PK WKS	PK POS	RANK	TITLE	ARTIST
7/10	4	1	1.	(I Can't Get No) Satisfaction	The Rolling Stones
10/09	4	1	2.	Yesterday	The Beatles
12/04	3	1	3.	Turn! Turn! Turn! (To Everything There Is A Season)	The Byrds
5/01	3	1	4.	Mrs. Brown You've Got A Lovely Daughter	Herman's Hermits
8/14	3	1	5.	I Got You Babe	Sonny & Cher
9/04	3	1	6.	Help!	The Beatles
6/19	2	1	7.	I Can't Help Myself	Four Tops
2/06	2	1	8.	You've Lost That Lovin' Feelin'	The Righteous Brothers
1/23	2	1	9.	Downtown	Petula Clark
2/20	2	1	10.	This Diamond Ring	Gary Lewis & The Playboys
3/27	2	1	11.	Stop! In The Name Of Love	The Supremes
5/29	2	1	12.	Help Me, Rhonda	The Beach Boys
11/06	2	1	13.	Get Off Of My Cloud	The Rolling Stones
11/20	2	1	14.	I Hear A Symphony	The Supremes
4/10	2	1	15.	I'm Telling You Now	Freddie & The Dreamers
3/13	2	1	16.	Eight Days A Week	The Beatles
3/06	1	1	17.	My Girl	The Temptations
10/02	1	1	18.	Hang On Sloopy	The McCoys
6/26	1	1	19.	Mr. Tambourine Man	The Byrds
9/25	1	1	20.	Eve Of Destruction	Barry McGuire
12/25	1	1	21.	Over And Over	The Dave Clark Five
5/22	1	1	22.	Ticket To Ride	The Beatles
8/07	1	1	23.	I'm Henry VIII, I Am	Herman's Hermits
4/24	1	1	24.	Game Of Love	Wayne Fontana/The Mindbenders
6/12	1	1	25.	Back In My Arms Again	The Supremes
10/30	3	2	26.	A Lover's Concerto	The Toys
6/05	2	2	27.	Wooly Bully	Sam The Sham & The Pharoahs
3/27	2	2	28.	Can't You Hear My Heartbeat	Herman's Hermits
9/04	2	2	29.	Like A Rolling Stone	Bob Dylan
10/16	2	2	30.	Treat Her Right	Roy Head & The Traits
5/08	2	2	31.	Count Me In	Gary Lewis & The Playboys
11/20	1	2	32.	1-2-3	Len Barry
8/21	1	2	33.	Save Your Heart For Me	Gary Lewis & The Playboys
12/18	3	3	34.	I Got You (I Feel Good)	James Brown
3/20	2	3	35.	The Birds And The Bees	Jewel Akens
1/16	2	3	36.	Love Potion Number Nine	The Searchers
1/30	2	3	37.	The Name Game	Shirley Ellis
7/31	2	3	38.	What's New Pussycat?	Tom Jones
8/28	2	3	39.	California Girls	The Beach Boys
12/11	1	3	40.	Let's Hang On!	The 4 Seasons

TOP 40 HITS
1966

PK DATE	PK WKS	PK POS	RANK	TITLE	ARTIST
12/31	7	1	1.	I'm A Believer	The Monkees
3/05	5	1	2.	The Ballad Of The Green Berets	SSgt Barry Sadler
12/03	3	1	3.	Winchester Cathedral	The New Vaudeville Band
4/09	3	1	4.	(You're My) Soul And Inspiration	The Righteous Brothers
5/07	3	1	5.	Monday, Monday	The Mama's & The Papa's
1/08	3	1	6.	We Can Work It Out	The Beatles
8/13	3	1	7.	Summer In The City	The Lovin' Spoonful
9/24	3	1	8.	Cherish	The Association
9/10	2	1	9.	You Can't Hurry Love	The Supremes
7/30	2	1	10.	Wild Thing	The Troggs
10/15	2	1	11.	Reach Out I'll Be There	Four Tops
6/11	2	1	12.	Paint It, Black	The Rolling Stones
5/28	2	1	13.	When A Man Loves A Woman	Percy Sledge
11/19	2	1	14.	You Keep Me Hangin' On	The Supremes
7/16	2	1	15.	Hanky Panky	Tommy James & The Shondells
2/05	2	1	16.	My Love	Petula Clark
1/01	2	1	17.	The Sounds Of Silence	Simon & Garfunkel
6/25	2	1	18.	Paperback Writer	The Beatles
10/29	1	1	19.	96 Tears	? & The Mysterians
11/05	1	1	20.	Last Train To Clarksville	The Monkees
11/12	1	1	21.	Poor Side Of Town	Johnny Rivers
2/26	1	1	22.	These Boots Are Made For Walkin'	Nancy Sinatra
12/10	1	1	23.	Good Vibrations	The Beach Boys
4/30	1	1	24.	Good Lovin'	The Young Rascals
7/02	1	1	25.	Strangers In The Night	Frank Sinatra
9/03	1	1	26.	Sunshine Superman	Donovan
2/19	1	1	27.	Lightnin' Strikes	Lou Christie
12/31	4	2	28.	Snoopy Vs. The Red Baron	The Royal Guardsmen
12/10	3	2	29.	Mellow Yellow	Donovan
3/19	3	2	30.	19th Nervous Breakdown	The Rolling Stones
8/06	2	2	31.	Lil' Red Riding Hood	Sam The Sham & The Pharoahs
4/09	2	2	32.	Daydream	The Lovin' Spoonful
8/20	2	2	33.	Sunny	Bobby Hebb
6/11	2	2	34.	Did You Ever Have To Make Up Your Mind?	The Lovin' Spoonful
5/28	2	2	35.	A Groovy Kind Of Love	The Mindbenders
1/29	2	2	36.	Barbara Ann	The Beach Boys
7/09	1	2	37.	Red Rubber Ball	The Cyrkle
4/23	1	2	38.	Bang Bang (My Baby Shot Me Down)	Cher
9/17	1	2	39.	Yellow Submarine	The Beatles
5/21	1	2	40.	Rainy Day Women #12 & 35	Bob Dylan

TOP 40 HITS
1967

PK DATE	PK WKS	PK POS	RANK	TITLE	ARTIST
10/21	5	1	1.	To Sir With Love	Lulu
12/02	4	1	2.	Daydream Believer	The Monkees
7/01	4	1	3.	Windy	The Association
8/26	4	1	4.	Ode To Billie Joe	Bobbie Gentry
4/15	4	1	5.	Somethin' Stupid	Nancy Sinatra & Frank Sinatra
5/20	4	1	6.	Groovin'	The Young Rascals
9/23	4	1	7.	The Letter	The Box Tops
7/29	3	1	8.	Light My Fire	The Doors
3/25	3	1	9.	Happy Together	The Turtles
12/30	3	1	10.	Hello Goodbye	The Beatles
6/03	2	1	11.	Respect	Aretha Franklin
2/18	2	1	12.	Kind Of A Drag	The Buckinghams
11/25	1	1	13.	Incense And Peppermints	Strawberry Alarm Clock
3/11	1	1	14.	Love Is Here And Now You're Gone	The Supremes
3/04	1	1	15.	Ruby Tuesday	The Rolling Stones
8/19	1	1	16.	All You Need Is Love	The Beatles
5/13	1	1	17.	The Happening	The Supremes
3/18	1	1	18.	Penny Lane	The Beatles
12/16	3	2	19.	I Heard It Through The Grapevine	Gladys Knight & The Pips
11/04	3	2	20.	Soul Man	Sam & Dave
3/25	3	2	21.	Dedicated To The One I Love	The Mamas & The Papas
7/08	2	2	22.	Little Bit O' Soul	The Music Explosion
12/02	2	2	23.	The Rain, The Park & Other Things	The Cowsills
2/04	2	2	24.	Georgy Girl	The Seekers
10/07	2	2	25.	Never My Love	The Association
7/29	2	2	26.	I Was Made To Love Her	Stevie Wonder
9/09	2	2	27.	Reflections	Diana Ross & The Supremes
7/22	1	2	28.	Can't Take My Eyes Off You	Frankie Valli
1/28	1	2	29.	Tell It Like It Is	Aaron Neville
5/13	1	2	30.	Sweet Soul Music	Arthur Conley
4/29	1	2	31.	A Little Bit Me, A Little Bit You	The Monkees
9/09	3	3	32.	Come Back When You Grow Up	Bobby Vee
5/27	3	3	33.	I Got Rhythm	The Happenings
11/04	2	3	34.	It Must Be Him	Vikki Carr
8/19	2	3	35.	Pleasant Valley Sunday	The Monkees
3/11	2	3	36.	Baby I Need Your Lovin'	Johnny Rivers
6/17	2	3	37.	She'd Rather Be With Me	The Turtles
4/15	1	3	38.	This Is My Song	Petula Clark
5/27	4	4	39.	Release Me (And Let Me Love Again)	Engelbert Humperdinck
7/01	4	4	40.	San Francisco (Be Sure To Wear Flowers In Your Hair)	Scott McKenzie

TOP 40 HITS
1968

PK DATE	PK WKS	PK POS	RANK	TITLE	ARTIST
9/28	9	1	1.	Hey Jude	The Beatles
12/14	7	1	2.	I Heard It Through The Grapevine	Marvin Gaye
2/10	5	1	3.	Love Is Blue	Paul Mauriat
4/13	5	1	4.	Honey	Bobby Goldsboro
8/17	5	1	5.	People Got To Be Free	The Rascals
3/16	4	1	6.	(Sittin' On) The Dock Of The Bay	Otis Redding
6/22	4	1	7.	This Guy's In Love With You	Herb Alpert
6/01	3	1	8.	Mrs. Robinson	Simon & Garfunkel
11/30	2	1	9.	Love Child	Diana Ross & The Supremes
5/18	2	1	10.	Tighten Up	Archie Bell & The Drells
8/03	2	1	11.	Hello, I Love You	The Doors
1/20	2	1	12.	Judy In Disguise (With Glasses)	John Fred & His Playboy Band
7/20	2	1	13.	Grazing In The Grass	Hugh Masekela
9/21	1	1	14.	Harper Valley P.T.A.	Jeannie C. Riley
2/03	1	1	15.	Green Tambourine	The Lemon Pipers
2/24	4	2	16.	(Theme From) Valley Of The Dolls	Dionne Warwick
4/06	3	2	17.	Young Girl	Union Gap feat. Gary Puckett
11/02	3	2	18.	Those Were The Days	Mary Hopkin
6/29	3	2	19.	The Horse	Cliff Nobles & Co.
8/24	3	2	20.	Born To Be Wild	Steppenwolf
12/28	2	2	21.	For Once In My Life	Stevie Wonder
1/20	2	2	22.	Chain Of Fools	Aretha Franklin
4/27	2	2	23.	Cry Like A Baby	The Box Tops
8/03	2	2	24.	Classical Gas	Mason Williams
7/20	2	2	25.	Lady Willpower	Gary Puckett & The Union Gap
10/26	1	2	26.	Little Green Apples	O.C. Smith
6/01	1	2	27.	The Good, The Bad And The Ugly	Hugo Montenegro
10/19	1	2	28.	Fire	The Crazy World Of Arthur Brown
6/22	1	2	29.	MacArthur Park	Richard Harris
7/27	3	3	30.	Stoned Soul Picnic	The 5th Dimension
2/10	3	3	31.	Spooky	Classics IV
7/06	3	3	32.	Jumpin' Jack Flash	The Rolling Stones
8/31	3	3	33.	Light My Fire	Jose Feliciano
5/25	2	3	34.	A Beautiful Morning	The Rascals
3/30	2	3	35.	Valleri	The Monkees
11/30	1	3	36.	Magic Carpet Ride	Steppenwolf
6/15	1	3	37.	Mony Mony	Tommy James & The Shondells
3/09	4	4	38.	Simon Says	1910 Fruitgum Co.
1/13	3	4	39.	Woman, Woman	Union Gap feat. Gary Puckett
2/17	3	4	40.	I Wish It Would Rain	The Temptations

TOP 40 HITS
1969

PK DATE	PK WKS	PK POS	RANK	TITLE	ARTIST
4/12	6	1	1.	Aquarius/Let The Sunshine In	The 5th Dimension
7/12	6	1	2.	In The Year 2525 (Exordium & Terminus)	Zager & Evans
5/24	5	1	3.	Get Back	The Beatles with Billy Preston
9/20	4	1	4.	Sugar, Sugar	The Archies
8/23	4	1	5.	Honky Tonk Women	The Rolling Stones
2/15	4	1	6.	Everyday People	Sly & The Family Stone
3/15	4	1	7.	Dizzy	Tommy Roe
11/08	3	1	8.	Wedding Bell Blues	The 5th Dimension
10/18	2	1	9.	I Can't Get Next To You	The Temptations
2/01	2	1	10.	Crimson And Clover	Tommy James & The Shondells
12/06	2	1	11.	Na Na Hey Hey Kiss Him Goodbye	Steam
6/28	2	1	12.	Love Theme From Romeo & Juliet	Henry Mancini
12/20	1	1	13.	Leaving On A Jet Plane	Peter, Paul & Mary
11/29	1	1	14.	Come Together	The Beatles
12/27	1	1	15.	Someday We'll Be Together	Diana Ross & The Supremes
11/01	1	1	16.	Suspicious Minds	Elvis Presley
7/26	3	2	17.	Crystal Blue Persuasion	Tommy James & The Shondells
3/08	3	2	18.	Proud Mary	Creedence Clearwater Revival
7/05	3	2	19.	Spinning Wheel	Blood, Sweat & Tears
8/23	3	2	20.	A Boy Named Sue	Johnny Cash
4/12	3	2	21.	You've Made Me So Very Happy	Blood, Sweat & Tears
5/10	2	2	22.	Hair	The Cowsills
1/11	2	2	23.	I'm Gonna Make You Love Me	Supremes & Temptations
10/18	2	2	24.	Hot Fun In The Summertime	Sly & The Family Stone
10/04	2	2	25.	Jean	Oliver
5/31	2	2	26.	Love (Can Make You Happy)	Mercy
9/27	1	2	27.	Green River	Creedence Clearwater Revival
11/22	1	2	28.	Take A Letter Maria	R.B. Greaves
5/03	1	2	29.	It's Your Thing	The Isley Brothers
11/29	1	2	30.	And When I Die	Blood, Sweat & Tears
6/28	1	2	31.	Bad Moon Rising	Creedence Clearwater Revival
3/29	1	2	32.	Traces	Classics IV Featuring Dennis Yost
2/22	3	3	33.	Build Me Up Buttercup	The Foundations
10/04	2	3	34.	Little Woman	Bobby Sherman
2/01	2	3	35.	Worst That Could Happen	Brooklyn Bridge
3/29	2	3	36.	Time Of The Season	The Zombies
7/12	2	3	37.	Good Morning Starshine	Oliver
11/15	2	3	38.	Something	The Beatles
1/11	1	3	39.	Wichita Lineman	Glen Campbell
12/20	1	3	40.	Down On The Corner	Creedence Clearwater Revival

TOP 40 HITS
1970

PK DATE	PK WKS	PK POS	RANK	TITLE	ARTIST
2/28	6	1	1.	Bridge Over Troubled Water	Simon & Garfunkel
10/17	5	1	2.	I'll Be There	The Jackson 5
1/03	4	1	3.	Raindrops Keep Fallin' On My Head	B.J. Thomas
7/25	4	1	4.	(They Long To Be) Close To You	Carpenters
12/26	4	1	5.	My Sweet Lord	George Harrison
11/21	3	1	6.	I Think I Love You	The Partridge Family
9/19	3	1	7.	Ain't No Mountain High Enough	Diana Ross
5/09	3	1	8.	American Woman	The Guess Who
8/29	3	1	9.	War	Edwin Starr
4/11	2	1	10.	Let It Be	The Beatles
12/12	2	1	11.	The Tears Of A Clown	Smokey Robinson & The Miracles
7/11	2	1	12.	Mama Told Me (Not To Come)	Three Dog Night
4/25	2	1	13.	ABC	The Jackson 5
6/27	2	1	14.	The Love You Save	The Jackson 5
2/14	2	1	15.	Thank You (Falettinme Be Mice Elf Agin)	Sly & The Family Stone
5/30	2	1	16.	Everything Is Beautiful	Ray Stevens
6/13	2	1	17.	The Long And Winding Road	The Beatles
8/22	1	1	18.	Make It With You	Bread
1/31	1	1	19.	I Want You Back	The Jackson 5
2/07	1	1	20.	Venus	The Shocking Blue
10/10	1	1	21.	Cracklin' Rosie	Neil Diamond
10/31	4	2	22.	We've Only Just Begun	Carpenters
12/26	2	2	23.	One Less Bell To Answer	The 5th Dimension
6/06	2	2	24.	Which Way You Goin' Billy?	The Poppy Family/Susan Jacks
3/07	2	2	25.	Travelin' Band	Creedence Clearwater Revival
10/03	1	2	26.	Lookin' Out My Back Door	Creedence Clearwater Revival
2/21	1	2	27.	Hey There Lonely Girl	Eddie Holman
3/21	1	2	28.	The Rapper	The Jaggerz
5/23	1	2	29.	Vehicle	The Ides Of March
6/27	3	3	30.	Ball Of Confusion (That's What The World Is Today)	The Temptations
10/31	3	3	31.	Fire And Rain	James Taylor
4/18	3	3	32.	Spirit In The Sky	Norman Greenbaum
3/28	3	3	33.	Instant Karma (We All Shine On)	John Ono Lennon
12/05	2	3	34.	Gypsy Woman	Brian Hyland
10/03	2	3	35.	Candida	Dawn
10/17	2	3	36.	Green-Eyed Lady	Sugarloaf
8/08	2	3	37.	Signed, Sealed, Delivered I'm Yours	Stevie Wonder
5/30	2	3	38.	Love On A Two-Way Street	The Moments
7/25	1	3	39.	Band Of Gold	Freda Payne
8/22	1	3	40.	Spill The Wine	Eric Burdon & War

TOP 40 HITS
1971

PK DATE	PK WKS	PK POS	RANK	TITLE	ARTIST
4/17	6	1	1.	Joy To The World	Three Dog Night
10/02	5	1	2.	Maggie May	Rod Stewart
6/19	5	1	3.	It's Too Late	Carole King
2/13	5	1	4.	One Bad Apple	The Osmonds
8/07	4	1	5.	How Can You Mend A Broken Heart	The Bee Gees
1/23	3	1	6.	Knock Three Times	Dawn
12/25	3	1	7.	Brand New Key	Melanie
9/11	3	1	8.	Go Away Little Girl	Donny Osmond
12/04	3	1	9.	Family Affair	Sly & The Family Stone
11/06	2	1	10.	Gypsys, Tramps & Thieves	Cher
4/03	2	1	11.	Just My Imagination (Running Away With Me)	The Temptations
11/20	2	1	12.	Theme From Shaft	Isaac Hayes
3/20	2	1	13.	Me And Bobby McGee	Janis Joplin
5/29	2	1	14.	Brown Sugar	The Rolling Stones
7/24	1	1	15.	Indian Reservation	Raiders
6/12	1	1	16.	Want Ads	The Honey Cone
7/31	1	1	17.	You've Got A Friend	James Taylor
9/04	1	1	18.	Uncle Albert/Admiral Halsey	Paul & Linda McCartney
4/10	3	2	19.	What's Going On	Marvin Gaye
5/08	3	2	20.	Never Can Say Goodbye	The Jackson 5
8/14	2	2	21.	Mr. Big Stuff	Jean Knight
10/16	2	2	22.	Superstar	Carpenters
6/19	2	2	23.	Rainy Days And Mondays	Carpenters
9/11	2	2	24.	Spanish Harlem	Aretha Franklin
2/27	2	2	25.	Mama's Pearl	The Jackson 5
8/28	1	2	26.	Take Me Home, Country Roads	John Denver
3/20	1	2	27.	She's A Lady	Tom Jones
5/01	1	2	28.	Put Your Hand In The Hand	Ocean
10/16	3	3	29.	Yo-Yo	The Osmonds
12/11	2	3	30.	Have You Seen Her	Chi-Lites
7/03	2	3	31.	Treat Her Like A Lady	Cornelius Brothers & Sister Rose
3/13	2	3	32.	For All We Know	Carpenters
2/13	2	3	33.	Rose Garden	Lynn Anderson
9/04	2	3	34.	Smiling Faces Sometimes	The Undisputed Truth
9/18	2	3	35.	Ain't No Sunshine	Bill Withers
11/13	2	3	36.	Imagine	John Lennon Plastic Ono Band
11/27	2	3	37.	Baby I'm-A Want You	Bread
10/02	1	3	38.	The Night They Drove Old Dixie Down	Joan Baez
1/30	1	3	39.	Lonely Days	Bee Gees
8/28	1	3	40.	Signs	Five Man Electrical Band

TOP 40 HITS
1972

PK DATE	PK WKS	PK POS	RANK	TITLE	ARTIST
4/15	6	1	1.	The First Time Ever I Saw Your Face	Roberta Flack
7/29	6	1	2.	Alone Again (Naturally)	Gilbert O'Sullivan
1/15	4	1	3.	American Pie - Parts I & II	Don McLean
2/19	4	1	4.	Without You	Nilsson
11/04	4	1	5.	I Can See Clearly Now	Johnny Nash
3/25	3	1	6.	A Horse With No Name	America
9/23	3	1	7.	Baby Don't Get Hooked On Me	Mac Davis
12/16	3	1	8.	Me And Mrs. Jones	Billy Paul
6/10	3	1	9.	The Candy Man	Sammy Davis, Jr.
7/08	3	1	10.	Lean On Me	Bill Withers
10/21	2	1	11.	My Ding-A-Ling	Chuck Berry
8/26	1	1	12.	Brandy (You're A Fine Girl)	Looking Glass
2/12	1	1	13.	Let's Stay Together	Al Green
12/09	1	1	14.	I Am Woman	Helen Reddy
6/03	1	1	15.	I'll Take You There	The Staple Singers
3/18	1	1	16.	Heart Of Gold	Neil Young
5/27	1	1	17.	Oh Girl	Chi-Lites
10/14	1	1	18.	Ben	Michael Jackson
12/02	1	1	19.	Papa Was A Rollin' Stone	The Temptations
7/01	1	1	20.	Song Sung Blue	Neil Diamond
9/16	1	1	21.	Black & White	Three Dog Night
5/06	2	2	22.	I Gotcha	Joe Tex
9/02	2	2	23.	Long Cool Woman (In A Black Dress)	The Hollies
7/15	2	2	24.	Too Late To Turn Back Now	Cornelius Brothers & Sister Rose
4/22	2	2	25.	Rockin' Robin	Michael Jackson
11/04	2	2	26.	Nights In White Satin	The Moody Blues
12/30	2	2	27.	Clair	Gilbert O'Sullivan
2/26	2	2	28.	Hurting Each Other	Carpenters
11/18	2	2	29.	I'd Love You To Want Me	Lobo
10/14	2	2	30.	Use Me	Bill Withers
7/08	1	2	31.	Outa-Space	Billy Preston
10/28	1	2	32.	Burning Love	Elvis Presley
3/11	3	3	33.	The Lion Sleeps Tonight	Robert John
8/05	2	3	34.	(If Loving You Is Wrong) I Don't Want To Be Right	Luther Ingram
2/26	2	3	35.	Precious And Few	Climax
12/23	2	3	36.	You Ought To Be With Me	Al Green
9/02	2	3	37.	I'm Still In Love With You	Al Green
12/09	2	3	38.	If You Don't Know Me By Now	Harold Melvin & The Bluenotes
11/18	2	3	39.	I'll Be Around	The Spinners
9/23	2	3	40.	Saturday In The Park	Chicago

TOP 40 HITS
1973

PK DATE	PK WKS	PK POS	RANK	TITLE	ARTIST
2/24	5	1	1.	Killing Me Softly With His Song	Roberta Flack
4/21	4	1	2.	Tie A Yellow Ribbon Round The Ole Oak Tree	Dawn Featuring Tony Orlando
6/02	4	1	3.	My Love	Paul McCartney & Wings
1/06	3	1	4.	You're So Vain	Carly Simon
2/03	3	1	5.	Crocodile Rock	Elton John
9/08	2	1	6.	Let's Get It On	Marvin Gaye
11/10	2	1	7.	Keep On Truckin' (Part 1)	Eddie Kendricks
7/21	2	1	8.	Bad, Bad Leroy Brown	Jim Croce
12/01	2	1	9.	Top Of The World	Carpenters
10/27	2	1	10.	Midnight Train To Georgia	Gladys Knight & The Pips
8/25	2	1	11.	Brother Louie	Stories
7/07	2	1	12.	Will It Go Round In Circles	Billy Preston
10/06	2	1	13.	Half-Breed	Cher
4/07	2	1	14.	The Night The Lights Went Out In Georgia	Vicki Lawrence
12/29	2	1	15.	Time In A Bottle	Jim Croce
12/15	2	1	16.	The Most Beautiful Girl	Charlie Rich
8/04	2	1	17.	The Morning After	Maureen McGovern
8/18	1	1	18.	Touch Me In The Morning	Diana Ross
9/15	1	1	19.	Delta Dawn	Helen Reddy
5/26	1	1	20.	Frankenstein	The Edgar Winter Group
5/19	1	1	21.	You Are The Sunshine Of My Life	Stevie Wonder
10/20	1	1	22.	Angie	The Rolling Stones
6/30	1	1	23.	Give Me Love - (Give Me Peace On Earth)	George Harrison
9/29	1	1	24.	We're An American Band	Grand Funk
1/27	1	1	25.	Superstition	Stevie Wonder
3/24	1	1	26.	Love Train	O'Jays
11/24	1	1	27.	Photograph	Ringo Starr
2/24	4	2	28.	Dueling Banjos	Eric Weissberg & Steve Mandell
12/08	3	2	29.	Goodbye Yellow Brick Road	Elton John
8/11	3	2	30.	Live And Let Die	Wings
6/16	2	2	31.	Playground In My Mind	Clint Holmes
7/07	2	2	32.	Kodachrome	Paul Simon
4/07	2	2	33.	Neither One Of Us (Wants To Be The First To Say Goodbye)	Gladys Knight & The Pips
4/28	2	2	34.	The Cisco Kid	War
10/06	1	2	35.	Loves Me Like A Rock	Paul Simon
6/02	1	2	36.	Daniel	Elton John
10/13	1	2	37.	Ramblin Man	The Allman Brothers Band
7/28	1	2	38.	Yesterday Once More	Carpenters
3/31	1	2	39.	Also Sprach Zarathustra (2001)	Deodato
5/05	3	3	40.	Little Willy	The Sweet

TOP 40 HITS
1974

PK DATE	PK WKS	PK POS	RANK	TITLE	ARTIST
2/02	3	1	1.	The Way We Were	Barbra Streisand
3/02	3	1	2.	Seasons In The Sun	Terry Jacks
5/18	3	1	3.	The Streak	Ray Stevens
8/24	3	1	4.	(You're) Having My Baby	Paul Anka
12/07	2	1	5.	Kung Fu Fighting	Carl Douglas
6/15	2	1	6.	Billy, Don't Be A Hero	Bo Donaldson & The Heywoods
7/27	2	1	7.	Annie's Song	John Denver
5/04	2	1	8.	The Loco-Motion..................................	Grand Funk
4/20	2	1	9.	TSOP (The Sound Of Philadelphia)	MFSB with The Three Degrees
11/23	2	1	10.	I Can Help..	Billy Swan
7/13	2	1	11.	Rock Your Baby....................................	George McCrae
10/05	2	1	12.	I Honestly Love You	Olivia Newton-John
4/13	1	1	13.	Bennie And The Jets	Elton John
1/12	1	1	14.	The Joker...	Steve Miller Band
10/26	1	1	15.	Then Came You	Dionne Warwicke & Spinners
2/09	1	1	16.	Love's Theme......................................	Love Unlimited Orchestra
1/19	1	1	17.	Show And Tell.....................................	Al Wilson
11/02	1	1	18.	You Haven't Done Nothin	Stevie Wonder
10/19	1	1	19.	Nothing From Nothing	Billy Preston
4/06	1	1	20.	Hooked On A Feeling	Blue Swede
3/30	1	1	21.	Sunshine On My Shoulders	John Denver
6/08	1	1	22.	Band On The Run	Paul McCartney & Wings
1/26	1	1	23.	You're Sixteen	Ringo Starr
6/29	1	1	24.	Sundown...	Gordon Lightfoot
9/28	1	1	25.	Rock Me Gently	Andy Kim
12/28	1	1	26.	Angie Baby..	Helen Reddy
8/10	1	1	27.	Feel Like Makin' Love	Roberta Flack
12/21	1	1	28.	Cat's In The Cradle...............................	Harry Chapin
3/23	1	1	29.	Dark Lady	Cher
8/17	1	1	30.	The Night Chicago Died	Paper Lace
11/09	1	1	31.	You Ain't Seen Nothing Yet.....................	Bachman-Turner Overdrive
7/06	1	1	32.	Rock The Boat	The Hues Corporation
9/14	1	1	33.	I Shot The Sheriff	Eric Clapton
9/21	1	1	34.	Can't Get Enough Of Your Love, Babe.........	Barry White
11/16	1	1	35.	Whatever Gets You Thru The Night	John Lennon/Plastic Ono Band
5/18	2	2	36.	Dancing Machine	The Jackson 5
6/15	2	2	37.	You Make Me Feel Brand New...................	The Stylistics
11/16	2	2	38.	Do It ('Til You're Satisfied)......................	B.T. Express
3/09	2	2	39.	Boogie Down	Eddie Kendricks
7/27	2	2	40.	Don't Let The Sun Go Down On Me	Elton John

TOP 40 HITS
1975

PK DATE	PK WKS	PK POS	RANK	TITLE	ARTIST
6/21	4	1	1.	Love Will Keep Us Together	The Captain & Tennille
11/29	3	1	2.	Fly, Robin, Fly	Silver Convention
11/01	3	1	3.	Island Girl	Elton John
5/03	3	1	4.	He Don't Love You (Like I Love You)	Tony Orlando & Dawn
10/11	3	1	5.	Bad Blood	Neil Sedaka
9/06	2	1	6.	Rhinestone Cowboy	Glen Campbell
4/12	2	1	7.	Philadelphia Freedom	The Elton John Band
11/22	2	1	8.	That's The Way (I Like It)	KC & The Sunshine Band
8/09	2	1	9.	Jive Talkin'	Bee Gees
9/20	2	1	10.	Fame	David Bowie
1/04	2	1	11.	Lucy In The Sky With Diamonds	Elton John
8/02	1	1	12.	One Of These Nights	Eagles
5/31	1	1	13.	Before The Next Teardrop Falls	Freddy Fender
3/22	1	1	14.	My Eyes Adored You	Frankie Valli
4/05	1	1	15.	Lovin' You	Minnie Riperton
2/01	1	1	16.	Laughter In The Rain	Neil Sedaka
4/26	1	1	17.	(Hey Won't You Play) Another Somebody Done Somebody Wrong Song	B.J. Thomas
3/29	1	1	18.	Lady Marmalade	LaBelle
2/22	1	1	19.	Pick Up The Pieces	AWB (Average White Band)
7/26	1	1	20.	The Hustle	Van McCoy
3/15	1	1	21.	Black Water	The Doobie Brothers
12/27	1	1	22.	Let's Do It Again	The Staple Singers
3/08	1	1	23.	Have You Never Been Mellow	Olivia Newton-John
7/19	1	1	24.	Listen To What The Man Said	Wings
3/01	1	1	25.	Best Of My Love	The Eagles
8/23	1	1	26.	Fallin' In Love	Hamilton, Joe Frank & Reynolds
6/07	1	1	27.	Thank God I'm A Country Boy	John Denver
5/24	1	1	28.	Shining Star	Earth, Wind & Fire
1/25	1	1	29.	Please Mr. Postman	Carpenters
1/18	1	1	30.	Mandy	Barry Manilow
2/15	1	1	31.	You're No Good	Linda Ronstadt
9/27	1	1	32.	I'm Sorry	John Denver
2/08	1	1	33.	Fire	Ohio Players
6/14	1	1	34.	Sister Golden Hair	America
8/30	1	1	35.	Get Down Tonight	K.C. & The Sunshine Band
10/11	4	2	36.	Calypso	John Denver
7/26	3	2	37.	I'm Not In Love	10cc
6/21	2	2	38.	When Will I Be Loved	Linda Ronstadt
1/04	2	2	39.	You're The First, The Last, My Everything	Barry White
11/08	2	2	40.	Lyin' Eyes	The Eagles

TOP 40 HITS
1976

PK DATE	PK WKS	PK POS	RANK	TITLE	ARTIST
11/13	8	1	1.	Tonight's The Night (Gonna Be Alright)	Rod Stewart
5/22	5	1	2.	Silly Love Songs	Wings
8/07	4	1	3.	Don't Go Breaking My Heart	Elton John & Kiki Dee
4/03	4	1	4.	Disco Lady	Johnnie Taylor
9/18	3	1	5.	Play That Funky Music	Wild Cherry
3/13	3	1	6.	December, 1963 (Oh, What a Night)	The Four Seasons
2/07	3	1	7.	50 Ways To Leave Your Lover	Paul Simon
7/24	2	1	8.	Kiss And Say Goodbye............................	Manhattans
10/23	2	1	9.	If You Leave Me Now............................	Chicago
5/29	2	1	10.	Love Hangover	Diana Ross
7/10	2	1	11.	Afternoon Delight................................	Starland Vocal Band
9/11	1	1	12.	(Shake, Shake, Shake) Shake Your Booty....	KC & The Sunshine Band
10/09	1	1	13.	A Fifth Of Beethoven............................	Walter Murphy/Big Apple Band
10/16	1	1	14.	Disco Duck (Part 1).............................	Rick Dees & His Cast Of Idiots
1/17	1	1	15.	I Write The Songs	Barry Manilow
1/31	1	1	16.	Love Rollercoaster	Ohio Players
5/15	1	1	17.	Boogie Fever	Sylvers
1/24	1	1	18.	Theme From Mahogany (Do You Know Where You're Going To)	Diana Ross
9/04	1	1	19.	You Should Be Dancing	Bee Gees
5/01	1	1	20.	Let Your Love Flow	Bellamy Brothers
1/10	1	1	21.	Convoy..	C.W. McCall
5/08	1	1	22.	Welcome Back.....................................	John Sebastian
3/06	1	1	23.	Love Machine (Part 1)	The Miracles
2/28	1	1	24.	Theme From S.W.A.T.	Rhythm Heritage
1/03	1	1	25.	Saturday Night....................................	Bay City Rollers
11/06	1	1	26.	Rock'n Me...	Steve Miller
12/04	3	2	27.	The Rubberband Man	Spinners
6/12	3	2	28.	Get Up And Boogie (That's Right).............	Silver Convention
3/27	3	2	29.	Dream Weaver	Gary Wright
3/06	3	2	30.	All By Myself......................................	Eric Carmen
9/25	2	2	31.	I'd Really Love To See You Tonight............	England Dan & John Ford Coley
5/01	2	2	32.	Right Back Where We Started From	Maxine Nightingale
9/04	2	2	33.	You'll Never Find Another Love Like Mine ...	Lou Rawls
7/31	2	2	34.	Love Is Alive......................................	Gary Wright
2/07	2	2	35.	Love To Love You Baby	Donna Summer
11/20	2	2	36.	The Wreck Of The Edmund Fitzgerald	Gordon Lightfoot
11/20	4	3	37.	Love So Right	Bee Gees
6/12	4	3	38.	Misty Blue	Dorthy Moore
8/14	4	3	39.	Let 'Em In	Wings
2/07	3	3	40.	You Sexy Thing	Hot Chocolate

TOP 40 HITS
1977

PK DATE	PK WKS	PK POS	RANK	TITLE	ARTIST
10/15	10	1	1.	You Light Up My Life	Debby Boone
8/20	5	1	2.	Best Of My Love	Emotions
7/30	4	1	3.	I Just Want To Be Your Everything	Andy Gibb
12/24	3	1	4.	How Deep Is Your Love	Bee Gees
3/05	3	1	5.	Love Theme From "A Star Is Born" (Evergreen)	Barbra Streisand
5/21	3	1	6.	Sir Duke	Stevie Wonder
2/05	2	1	7.	Torn Between Two Lovers	Mary MacGregor
3/26	2	1	8.	Rich Girl	Daryl Hall & John Oates
10/01	2	1	9.	Star Wars Theme/Cantina Band	Meco
6/25	1	1	10.	Got To Give It Up (Pt. I)	Marvin Gaye
1/29	1	1	11.	Car Wash	Rose Royce
1/08	1	1	12.	You Don't Have To Be A Star (To Be In My Show)	Marilyn McCoo & Billy Davis, Jr.
4/23	1	1	13.	Don't Leave Me This Way	Thelma Houston
1/15	1	1	14.	You Make Me Feel Like Dancing	Leo Sayer
4/09	1	1	15.	Dancing Queen	Abba
4/30	1	1	16.	Southern Nights	Glen Campbell
2/19	1	1	17.	Blinded By The Light	Manfred Mann's Earth Band
5/07	1	1	18.	Hotel California	Eagles
1/22	1	1	19.	I Wish	Stevie Wonder
7/02	1	1	20.	Gonna Fly Now	Bill Conti
7/09	1	1	21.	Undercover Angel	Alan O'Day
5/14	1	1	22.	When I Need You	Leo Sayer
4/16	1	1	23.	Don't Give Up On Us	David Soul
6/18	1	1	24.	Dreams	Fleetwood Mac
2/26	1	1	25.	New Kid In Town	Eagles
7/16	1	1	26.	Da Doo Ron Ron	Shaun Cassidy
6/11	1	1	27.	I'm Your Boogie Man	KC & The Sunshine Band
7/23	1	1	28.	Looks Like We Made It	Barry Manilow
11/26	3	2	29.	Don't It Make My Brown Eyes Blue	Crystal Gayle
10/22	3	2	30.	Nobody Does It Better	Carly Simon
10/01	3	2	31.	Keep It Comin' Love	KC & The Sunshine Band
7/30	3	2	32.	I'm In You	Peter Frampton
11/12	2	2	33.	Boogie Nights	Heatwave
3/12	2	2	34.	Fly Like An Eagle	Steve Miller
9/17	2	2	35.	Float On	The Floaters
9/10	1	2	36.	(Your Love Has Lifted Me) Higher And Higher	Rita Coolidge
12/17	4	3	37.	Blue Bayou	Linda Ronstadt
1/29	2	3	38.	Dazz	Brick
10/22	2	3	39.	That's Rock 'N' Roll	Shaun Cassidy
9/24	2	3	40.	Don't Stop	Fleetwood Mac

TOP 40 HITS
1978

PK DATE	PK WKS	PK POS	RANK	TITLE	ARTIST
3/18	8	1	1.	Night Fever	Bee Gees
6/17	7	1	2.	Shadow Dancing	Andy Gibb
12/09	6	1	3.	Le Freak	Chic
2/04	4	1	4.	Stayin' Alive	Bee Gees
9/30	4	1	5.	Kiss You All Over	Exile
9/09	3	1	6.	Boogie Oogie Oogie	A Taste Of Honey
1/14	3	1	7.	Baby Come Back	Player
11/11	3	1	8.	MacArthur Park	Donna Summer
3/04	2	1	9.	(Love Is) Thicker Than Water	Andy Gibb
8/12	2	1	10.	Three Times A Lady	Commodores
12/02	2	1	11.	You Don't Bring Me Flowers	Barbra Streisand & Neil Diamond
8/26	2	1	12.	Grease	Frankie Valli
5/20	2	1	13.	With A Little Luck	Wings
5/13	1	1	14.	If I Can't Have You	Yvonne Elliman
10/28	1	1	15.	Hot Child In The City	Nick Gilder
6/10	1	1	16.	You're The One That I Want	John Travolta & Olivia Newton-John
8/05	1	1	17.	Miss You	The Rolling Stones
11/04	1	1	18.	You Needed Me	Anne Murray
6/03	1	1	19.	Too Much, Too Little, Too Late	Johnny Mathis/Deniece Williams
6/24	6	2	20.	Baker Street	Gerry Rafferty
1/28	3	2	21.	Short People	Randy Newman
5/13	2	2	22.	The Closer I Get To You	Roberta Flack with Donny Hathaway
11/18	2	2	23.	Double Vision	Foreigner
4/01	3	3	24.	Lay Down Sally	Eric Clapton
4/22	3	3	25.	Can't Smile Without You	Barry Manilow
11/18	3	3	26.	How Much I Feel	Ambrosia
3/18	2	3	27.	Emotion	Samantha Sang
2/18	2	3	28.	Just The Way You Are	Billy Joel
3/04	2	3	29.	Sometimes When We Touch	Dan Hill
9/23	2	3	30.	Hopelessly Devoted To You	Olivia Newton-John
7/08	2	3	31.	Take A Chance On Me	Abba
9/09	2	3	32.	Hot Blooded	Foreigner
8/12	2	3	33.	Last Dance	Donna Summer
10/28	2	3	34.	Reminiscing	Little River Band
6/24	2	3	35.	It's A Heartache	Bonnie Tyler
1/14	2	3	36.	Here You Come Again	Dolly Parton
2/04	3	4	37.	We Are The Champions	Queen
1/14	3	4	38.	You're In My Heart (The Final Acclaim)	Rod Stewart
12/09	2	4	39.	I Just Wanna Stop	Gino Vannelli
7/08	2	4	40.	Use Ta Be My Girl	The O'Jays

TOP 40 HITS
1979

PK DATE	PK WKS	PK POS	RANK	TITLE	ARTIST
8/25	6	1	1.	My Sharona	The Knack
7/14	5	1	2.	Bad Girls	Donna Summer
2/10	4	1	3.	Da Ya Think I'm Sexy?	Rod Stewart
5/05	4	1	4.	Reunited	Peaches & Herb
6/02	3	1	5.	Hot Stuff	Donna Summer
3/10	3	1	6.	I Will Survive	Gloria Gaynor
12/22	3	1	7.	Escape (The Pina Colada Song)	Rupert Holmes
6/30	2	1	8.	Ring My Bell	Anita Ward
12/08	2	1	9.	Babe	Styx
1/06	2	1	10.	Too Much Heaven	Bee Gees
10/20	2	1	11.	Rise	Herb Alpert
3/24	2	1	12.	Tragedy	Bee Gees
11/24	2	1	13.	No More Tears (Enough Is Enough)	Barbra Streisand/Donna Summer
11/17	1	1	14.	Still	Commodores
11/03	1	1	15.	Pop Muzik	M
10/06	1	1	16.	Sad Eyes	Robert John
4/14	1	1	17.	What A Fool Believes	The Doobie Brothers
8/18	1	1	18.	Good Times	Chic
11/10	1	1	19.	Heartache Tonight	Eagles
4/28	1	1	20.	Heart Of Glass	Blondie
4/21	1	1	21.	Knock On Wood	Amii Stewart
10/13	1	1	22.	Don't Stop 'Til You Get Enough	Michael Jackson
6/09	1	1	23.	Love You Inside Out	Bee Gees
2/03	3	2	24.	Y.M.C.A.	Village People
11/10	2	2	25.	Dim All The Lights	Donna Summer
9/15	2	2	26.	After The Love Has Gone	Earth, Wind & Fire
2/24	2	2	27.	Fire	Pointer Sisters
6/16	2	2	28.	We Are Family	Sister Sledge
8/11	4	3	29.	The Main Event/Fight	Barbra Streisand
1/06	3	3	30.	My Life	Billy Joel
2/17	2	3	31.	A Little More Love	Olivia Newton-John
9/15	2	3	32.	The Devil Went Down To Georgia	The Charlie Daniels Band
5/19	2	3	33.	In The Navy	Village People
5/05	1	3	34.	Music Box Dancer	Frank Mills
12/22	4	4	35.	Send One Your Love	Stevie Wonder
3/17	3	4	36.	Heaven Knows	Donna Summer with Brooklyn Dreams
5/12	2	4	37.	Stumblin' In	Suzi Quatro & Chris Norman
10/13	2	4	38.	Sail On	Commodores
4/07	2	4	39.	Sultans Of Swing	Dire Straits
6/16	2	4	40.	Just When I Needed You Most	Randy Vanwarmer

TOP 40 HITS
1980

PK DATE	PK WKS	PK POS	RANK	TITLE	ARTIST
11/15	6	1	1.	Lady	Kenny Rogers
4/19	6	1	2.	Call Me	Blondie
12/27	5	1	3.	(Just Like) Starting Over	John Lennon
9/06	4	1	4.	Upside Down	Diana Ross
3/22	4	1	5.	Another Brick In The Wall (Part II)	Pink Floyd
2/23	4	1	6.	Crazy Little Thing Called Love	Queen
1/19	4	1	7.	Rock With You	Michael Jackson
8/02	4	1	8.	Magic	Olivia Newton-John
5/31	4	1	9.	Funkytown	Lipps, Inc.
10/04	3	1	10.	Another One Bites The Dust	Queen
10/25	3	1	11.	Woman In Love	Barbra Streisand
6/28	3	1	12.	Coming Up (Live at Glasgow)	Paul McCartney & Wings
7/19	2	1	13.	It's Still Rock And Roll To Me	Billy Joel
2/16	1	1	14.	Do That To Me One More Time	The Captain & Tennille
1/05	1	1	15.	Please Don't Go	K.C. & The Sunshine Band
8/30	1	1	16.	Sailing	Christopher Cross
12/06	5	2	17.	More Than I Can Say	Leo Sayer
9/13	4	2	18.	All Out Of Love	Air Supply
4/26	4	2	19.	Ride Like The Wind	Christopher Cross
3/29	2	2	20.	Working My Way Back To You/Forgive Me, Girl	Spinners
3/01	2	2	21.	Yes, I'm Ready	Teri DeSario with K.C.
3/15	2	2	22.	Longer	Dan Fogelberg
7/19	4	3	23.	Little Jeannie	Elton John
1/26	4	3	24.	Coward Of The County	Kenny Rogers
5/03	4	3	25.	Lost In Love	Air Supply
6/28	3	3	26.	The Rose	Bette Midler
6/07	3	3	27.	Biggest Part Of Me	Ambrosia
11/15	3	3	28.	The Wanderer	Donna Summer
10/25	3	3	29.	He's So Shy	Pointer Sisters
9/06	2	3	30.	Emotional Rescue	The Rolling Stones
8/16	2	3	31.	Take Your Time (Do It Right) Part 1	The S.O.S. Band
3/08	4	4	32.	Desire	Andy Gibb
2/02	4	4	33.	Cruisin'	Smokey Robinson
4/19	4	4	34.	With You I'm Born Again	Billy Preston & Syreeta
7/19	3	4	35.	Cupid/I've Loved You For A Long Time	Spinners
5/24	3	4	36.	Don't Fall In Love With A Dreamer	Kenny Rogers with Kim Carnes
9/27	2	4	37.	Give Me The Night	George Benson
9/13	2	4	38.	Fame	Irene Cara
12/27	5	5	39.	Hungry Heart	Bruce Springsteen
12/06	3	5	40.	Master Blaster (Jammin')	Stevie Wonder

TOP 40 HITS
1981

PK DATE	PK WKS	PK POS	RANK	TITLE	ARTIST
11/21	10	1	1.	Physical	Olivia Newton-John
5/16	9	1	2.	Bette Davis Eyes	Kim Carnes
8/15	9	1	3.	Endless Love	Diana Ross & Lionel Richie
10/17	3	1	4.	Arthur's Theme (Best That You Can Do)	Christopher Cross
4/11	3	1	5.	Kiss On My List	Daryl Hall & John Oates
8/01	2	1	6.	Jessie's Girl	Rick Springfield
2/28	2	1	7.	I Love A Rainy Night	Eddie Rabbitt
2/21	2	1	8.	9 To 5	Dolly Parton
11/07	2	1	9.	Private Eyes	Daryl Hall & John Oates
3/28	2	1	10.	Rapture	Blondie
2/07	2	1	11.	Celebration	Kool & The Gang
5/02	2	1	12.	Morning Train (Nine To Five)	Sheena Easton
1/31	1	1	13.	The Tide Is High	Blondie
3/21	1	1	14.	Keep On Loving You	REO Speedwagon
6/20	1	1	15.	Stars on 45	Stars on 45
7/25	1	1	16.	The One That You Love	Air Supply
11/28	10	2	17.	Waiting For A Girl Like You	Foreigner
3/21	3	2	18.	Woman	John Lennon
10/31	3	2	19.	Start Me Up	The Rolling Stones
8/29	3	2	20.	Slow Hand	Pointer Sisters
5/02	3	2	21.	Just The Two Of Us	Grover Washington, Jr. with Bill Withers
1/10	3	2	22.	Love On The Rocks	Neil Diamond
5/23	3	2	23.	Being With You	Smokey Robinson
7/04	3	2	24.	All Those Years Ago	George Harrison
9/19	2	2	25.	Queen Of Hearts	Juice Newton
8/15	2	2	26.	Theme From "Greatest American Hero" (Believe It or Not)	Joey Scarbury
9/05	6	3	27.	Stop Draggin' My Heart Around	Stevie Nicks with Tom Petty & The Heartbreakers
12/19	5	3	28.	Let's Groove	Earth, Wind & Fire
3/21	4	3	29.	The Best Of Times	Styx
6/13	3	3	30.	Sukiyaki	A Taste Of Honey
8/15	2	3	31.	I Don't Need You	Kenny Rogers
1/10	2	3	32.	Guilty	Barbra Streisand & Barry Gibb
12/05	2	3	33.	Every Little Thing She Does Is Magic	The Police
9/05	4	4	34.	Urgent	Foreigner
5/02	4	4	35.	Angel Of The Morning	Juice Newton
10/17	4	4	36.	For Your Eyes Only	Sheena Easton
12/05	3	4	37.	Oh No	Commodores
10/03	2	4	38.	Who's Crying Now	Journey
6/20	2	4	39.	A Woman Needs Love (Just Like You Do)	Ray Parker Jr. & Raydio
9/05	5	5	40.	(There's) No Gettin' Over Me	Ronnie Milsap

TOP 40 HITS
1982

PK DATE	PK WKS	PK POS	RANK	TITLE	ARTIST
3/20	7	1	1.	I Love Rock 'N Roll	Joan Jett & The Blackhearts
5/15	7	1	2.	Ebony And Ivory	Paul McCartney/Stevie Wonder
7/24	6	1	3.	Eye Of The Tiger	Survivor
2/06	6	1	4.	Centerfold	The J. Geils Band
12/18	4	1	5.	Maneater	Daryl Hall & John Oates
10/02	4	1	6.	Jack & Diane	John Cougar
7/03	3	1	7.	Don't You Want Me	The Human League
11/06	3	1	8.	Up Where We Belong	Joe Cocker & Jennifer Warnes
9/04	2	1	9.	Abracadabra	The Steve Miller Band
9/11	2	1	10.	Hard To Say I'm Sorry	Chicago
11/27	2	1	11.	Truly	Lionel Richie
1/30	1	1	12.	I Can't Go For That (No Can Do)	Daryl Hall & John Oates
12/11	1	1	13.	Mickey	Toni Basil
10/30	1	1	14.	Who Can It Be Now?	Men At Work
5/08	1	1	15.	Chariots Of Fire - Titles	Vangelis
2/27	6	2	16.	Open Arms	Journey
7/03	5	2	17.	Rosanna	Toto
8/07	4	2	18.	Hurts So Good	John Cougar
5/22	4	2	19.	Don't Talk To Strangers	Rick Springfield
11/27	3	2	20.	Gloria	Laura Branigan
4/10	3	2	21.	We Got The Beat	Go-Go's
11/06	4	3	22.	Heart Attack	Olivia Newton-John
10/16	3	3	23.	Eye In The Sky	The Alan Parsons Project
5/22	3	3	24.	I've Never Been To Me	Charlene
2/13	2	3	25.	Harden My Heart	Quarterflash
7/24	7	4	26.	Hold Me	Fleetwood Mac
4/10	4	4	27.	Freeze-Frame	The J. Geils Band
3/20	3	4	28.	That Girl	Stevie Wonder
5/22	3	4	29.	867-5309/Jenny	Tommy Tutone
2/27	3	4	30.	Shake It Up	The Cars
10/23	3	4	31.	I Keep Forgettin' (Every Time You're Near)	Michael McDonald
6/26	3	4	32.	Heat Of The Moment	Asia
6/12	2	4	33.	The Other Woman	Ray Parker Jr.
11/13	4	5	34.	Heartlight	Neil Diamond
6/12	3	5	35.	Always On My Mind	Willie Nelson
9/18	3	5	36.	You Should Hear How She Talks About You	Melissa Manchester
4/03	3	5	37.	Make A Move On Me	Olivia Newton-John
9/04	2	5	38.	Even The Nights Are Better	Air Supply
3/20	2	5	39.	Sweet Dreams	Air Supply
7/17	2	5	40.	Let It Whip	Dazz Band

TOP 40 HITS
1983

PK DATE	PK WKS	PK POS	RANK	TITLE	ARTIST
7/09	8	1	1.	Every Breath You Take	The Police
3/05	7	1	2.	Billie Jean	Michael Jackson
5/28	6	1	3.	Flashdance...What A Feeling	Irene Cara
12/10	6	1	4.	Say Say Say	Paul McCartney & Michael Jackson
11/12	4	1	5.	All Night Long (All Night)	Lionel Richie
10/01	4	1	6.	Total Eclipse Of The Heart	Bonnie Tyler
1/15	4	1	7.	Down Under	Men At Work
4/30	3	1	8.	Beat It	Michael Jackson
10/29	2	1	9.	Islands In The Stream	Kenny Rogers & Dolly Parton
2/19	2	1	10.	Baby, Come To Me	Patti Austin with James Ingram
9/10	2	1	11.	Maniac	Michael Sembello
5/21	1	1	12.	Let's Dance	David Bowie
9/03	1	1	13.	Sweet Dreams (Are Made of This)	Eurythmics
9/24	1	1	14.	Tell Her About It	Billy Joel
2/05	1	1	15.	Africa	Toto
4/23	1	1	16.	Come On Eileen	Dexys Midnight Runners
7/02	5	2	17.	Electric Avenue	Eddy Grant
12/17	4	2	18.	Say It Isn't So	Daryl Hall - John Oates
2/26	4	2	19.	Shame On The Moon	Bob Seger/The Silver Bullet Band
1/08	3	2	20.	The Girl Is Mine	Michael Jackson/Paul McCartney
3/26	3	2	21.	Do You Really Want To Hurt Me	Culture Club
10/08	3	2	22.	Making Love Out Of Nothing At All	Air Supply
6/18	2	2	23.	Time (Clock Of The Heart)	Culture Club
5/07	1	2	24.	Jeopardy	Greg Kihn Band
11/12	5	3	25.	Uptown Girl	Billy Joel
9/10	4	3	26.	The Safety Dance	Men Without Hats
1/29	3	3	27.	Sexual Healing	Marvin Gaye
1/08	3	3	28.	Dirty Laundry	Don Henley
3/26	3	3	29.	Hungry Like The Wolf	Duran Duran
8/06	3	3	30.	She Works Hard For The Money	Donna Summer
12/24	3	3	31.	Union Of The Snake	Duran Duran
2/26	3	3	32.	Stray Cat Strut	Stray Cats
4/16	2	3	33.	Mr. Roboto	Styx
10/08	2	3	34.	King Of Pain	The Police
6/04	1	3	35.	Overkill	Men At Work
7/09	4	4	36.	Never Gonna Let You Go	Sergio Mendes
10/08	4	4	37.	True	Spandau Ballet
9/03	2	4	38.	Puttin' On The Ritz	Taco
3/26	2	4	39.	You Are	Lionel Richie
11/05	1	4	40.	One Thing Leads To Another	The Fixx

TOP 40 HITS
1984

PK DATE	PK WKS	PK POS	RANK	TITLE	ARTIST
12/22	6	1	1.	Like A Virgin	Madonna
7/07	5	1	2.	When Doves Cry	Prince
2/25	5	1	3.	Jump	Van Halen
3/31	3	1	4.	Footloose	Kenny Loggins
9/01	3	1	5.	What's Love Got To Do With It	Tina Turner
4/21	3	1	6.	Against All Odds (Take A Look At Me Now)	Phil Collins
10/13	3	1	7.	I Just Called To Say I Love You	Stevie Wonder
8/11	3	1	8.	Ghostbusters	Ray Parker Jr.
2/04	3	1	9.	Karma Chameleon	Culture Club
11/17	3	1	10.	Wake Me Up Before You Go-Go	Wham!
5/12	2	1	11.	Hello	Lionel Richie
1/21	2	1	12.	Owner Of A Lonely Heart	Yes
12/08	2	1	13.	Out Of Touch	Daryl Hall John Oates
6/09	2	1	14.	Time After Time	Cyndi Lauper
5/26	2	1	15.	Let's Hear It For The Boy	Deniece Williams
9/29	2	1	16.	Let's Go Crazy	Prince & The Revolution
6/23	2	1	17.	The Reflex	Duran Duran
11/03	2	1	18.	Caribbean Queen (No More Love On The Run)	Billy Ocean
9/22	1	1	19.	Missing You	John Waite
6/30	4	2	20.	Dancing In The Dark	Bruce Springsteen
12/15	4	2	21.	The Wild Boys	Duran Duran
3/24	3	2	22.	Somebody's Watching Me	Rockwell
3/10	2	2	23.	Girls Just Want To Have Fun	Cyndi Lauper
11/17	2	2	24.	Purple Rain	Prince & The Revolution
2/11	1	2	25.	Joanna	Kool & The Gang
3/03	1	2	26.	99 Luftballons	Nena
11/24	3	3	27.	I Feel For You	Chaka Khan
9/08	3	3	28.	She Bop	Cyndi Lauper
1/28	3	3	29.	Talking In Your Sleep	The Romantics
9/29	3	3	30.	Drive	The Cars
8/04	3	3	31.	State Of Shock	Jacksons
7/07	2	3	32.	Jump (For My Love)	Pointer Sisters
5/05	2	3	33.	Hold Me Now	Thompson Twins
8/25	2	3	34.	Stuck On You	Lionel Richie
10/20	2	3	35.	Hard Habit To Break	Chicago
6/09	1	3	36.	Oh Sherrie	Steve Perry
3/31	2	4	37.	Here Comes The Rain Again	Eurythmics
6/30	2	4	38.	Self Control	Laura Branigan
7/14	2	4	39.	Eyes Without A Face	Billy Idol
3/03	2	4	40.	Thriller	Michael Jackson

TOP 40 HITS
1985

PK DATE	PK WKS	PK POS	RANK	TITLE	ARTIST
12/21	4	1	1.	Say You, Say Me	Lionel Richie
4/13	4	1	2.	We Are The World	USA for Africa
2/16	3	1	3.	Careless Whisper	Wham! Featuring George Michael
3/09	3	1	4.	Can't Fight This Feeling	REO Speedwagon
9/21	3	1	5.	Money For Nothing	Dire Straits
8/03	3	1	6.	Shout	Tears For Fears
12/07	2	1	7.	Broken Wings	Mr. Mister
2/02	2	1	8.	I Want To Know What Love Is	Foreigner
8/24	2	1	9.	The Power Of Love	Huey Lewis & The News
6/08	2	1	10.	Everybody Wants To Rule The World	Tears For Fears
11/16	2	1	11.	We Built This City	Starship
9/07	2	1	12.	St. Elmo's Fire (Man In Motion)	John Parr
5/25	2	1	13.	Everything She Wants	Wham!
6/22	2	1	14.	Heaven	Bryan Adams
7/13	2	1	15.	A View To A Kill	Duran Duran
3/30	2	1	16.	One More Night	Phil Collins
11/30	1	1	17.	Separate Lives	Phil Collins & Marilyn Martin
5/11	1	1	18.	Crazy For You	Madonna
7/27	1	1	19.	Everytime You Go Away	Paul Young
5/18	1	1	20.	Don't You (Forget About Me)	Simple Minds
11/02	1	1	21.	Part-Time Lover	Stevie Wonder
10/19	1	1	22.	Take On Me	a-ha
10/26	1	1	23.	Saving All My Love For You	Whitney Houston
11/09	1	1	24.	Miami Vice Theme	Jan Hammer
7/06	1	1	25.	Sussudio	Phil Collins
10/12	1	1	26.	Oh Sheila	Ready For The World
12/28	3	2	27.	Party All The Time	Eddie Murphy
9/21	3	2	28.	Cherish	Kool & The Gang
2/02	2	2	29.	Easy Lover	Philip Bailey/Phil Collins
11/16	2	2	30.	You Belong To The City	Glenn Frey
1/12	2	2	31.	All I Need	Jack Wagner
3/23	2	2	32.	Material Girl	Madonna
2/23	1	2	33.	Loverboy	Billy Ocean
7/20	1	2	34.	Raspberry Beret	Prince & The Revolution
3/16	1	2	35.	The Heat Is On	Glenn Frey
9/14	1	2	36.	We Don't Need Another Hero (Thunderdome)	Tina Turner
6/01	3	3	37.	Axel F	Harold Faltermeyer
4/27	2	3	38.	Rhythm Of The Night	DeBarge
12/28	2	3	39.	Alive & Kicking	Simple Minds
1/19	2	3	40.	You're The Inspiration	Chicago

TOP 40 HITS
1986

PK DATE	PK WKS	PK POS	RANK	TITLE	ARTIST
1/18	4	1	1.	That's What Friends Are For	Dionne & Friends
12/20	4	1	2.	Walk Like An Egyptian	Bangles
6/14	3	1	3.	On My Own	Patti LaBelle & Michael McDonald
5/17	3	1	4.	Greatest Love Of All	Whitney Houston
9/20	3	1	5.	Stuck With You	Huey Lewis & The News
3/29	3	1	6.	Rock Me Amadeus	Falco
3/01	2	1	7.	Kyrie	Mr. Mister
4/19	2	1	8.	Kiss	Prince & The Revolution
8/16	2	1	9.	Papa Don't Preach	Madonna
2/15	2	1	10.	How Will I Know	Whitney Houston
8/02	2	1	11.	Glory Of Love	Peter Cetera
10/11	2	1	12.	When I Think Of You	Janet Jackson
10/25	2	1	13.	True Colors	Cyndi Lauper
11/08	2	1	14.	Amanda	Boston
12/13	1	1	15.	The Way It Is	Bruce Hornsby & The Range
11/22	1	1	16.	Human	Human League
5/03	1	1	17.	Addicted To Love	Robert Palmer
7/05	1	1	18.	There'll Be Sad Songs (To Make You Cry)	Billy Ocean
7/26	1	1	19.	Sledgehammer	Peter Gabriel
5/10	1	1	20.	West End Girls	Pet Shop Boys
9/13	1	1	21.	Take My Breath Away	Berlin
3/15	1	1	22.	Sara	Starship
9/06	1	1	23.	Venus	Bananarama
12/06	1	1	24.	The Next Time I Fall	Peter Cetera w/Amy Grant
11/29	1	1	25.	You Give Love A Bad Name	Bon Jovi
7/12	1	1	26.	Holding Back The Years	Simply Red
8/30	1	1	27.	Higher Love	Steve Winwood
3/22	1	1	28.	These Dreams	Heart
6/07	1	1	29.	Live To Tell	Madonna
7/19	1	1	30.	Invisible Touch	Genesis
10/18	3	2	31.	Typical Male	Tina Turner
9/13	2	2	32.	Dancing On The Ceiling	Lionel Richie
12/27	2	2	33.	Everybody Have Fun Tonight	Wang Chung
9/27	2	2	34.	Friends And Lovers	Gloria Loring & Carl Anderson
2/01	2	2	35.	Burning Heart	Survivor
7/26	1	2	36.	Danger Zone	Kenny Loggins
10/11	1	2	37.	Don't Forget Me (When I'm Gone)	Glass Tiger
2/15	1	2	38.	When The Going Gets Tough, The Tough Get Going	Billy Ocean
4/19	1	2	39.	Manic Monday	Bangles
11/08	1	2	40.	I Didn't Mean To Turn You On	Robert Palmer

TOP 40 HITS
1987

PK DATE	PK WKS	PK POS	RANK	TITLE	ARTIST
12/12	4	1	1.	Faith	George Michael
2/14	4	1	2.	Livin' On A Prayer	Bon Jovi
7/11	3	1	3.	Alone	Heart
5/16	3	1	4.	With Or Without You	U2
8/29	3	1	5.	La Bamba	Los Lobos
6/27	2	1	6.	I Wanna Dance With Somebody (Who Loves Me)	Whitney Houston
4/04	2	1	7.	Nothing's Gonna Stop Us Now	Starship
8/08	2	1	8.	I Still Haven't Found What I'm Looking For	U2
9/26	2	1	9.	Didn't We Almost Have It All	Whitney Houston
4/18	2	1	10.	I Knew You Were Waiting (For Me)	Aretha Franklin & George Michael
1/24	2	1	11.	At This Moment	Billy Vera & The Beaters
11/07	2	1	12.	I Think We're Alone Now	Tiffany
5/02	2	1	13.	(I Just) Died In Your Arms	Cutting Crew
3/21	2	1	14.	Lean On Me	Club Nouveau
10/24	2	1	15.	Bad	Michael Jackson
1/17	1	1	16.	Shake You Down	Gregory Abbott
10/10	1	1	17.	Here I Go Again	Whitesnake
6/13	1	1	18.	Always	Atlantic Starr
6/20	1	1	19.	Head To Toe	Lisa Lisa & Cult Jam
8/01	1	1	20.	Shakedown	Bob Seger
12/05	1	1	21.	Heaven Is A Place On Earth	Belinda Carlisle
11/28	1	1	22.	(I've Had) The Time Of My Life	Bill Medley & Jennifer Warnes
2/07	1	1	23.	Open Your Heart	Madonna
6/06	1	1	24.	You Keep Me Hangin' On	Kim Wilde
10/17	1	1	25.	Lost In Emotion	Lisa Lisa & Cult Jam
11/21	1	1	26.	Mony Mony "Live"	Billy Idol
3/14	1	1	27.	Jacob's Ladder	Huey Lewis & The News
8/22	1	1	28.	Who's That Girl	Madonna
9/19	1	1	29.	I Just Can't Stop Loving You	Michael Jackson/Siedah Garrett
5/02	4	2	30.	Looking For A New Love	Jody Watley
10/24	3	2	31.	Causing A Commotion	Madonna
1/17	2	2	32.	C'est La Vie	Robbie Nevil
4/25	1	2	33.	Don't Dream It's Over	Crowded House
12/19	1	2	34.	Is This Love	Whitesnake
8/08	1	2	35.	I Want Your Sex	George Michael
10/17	1	2	36.	U Got The Look	Prince
1/10	1	2	37.	Notorious	Duran Duran
2/21	1	2	38.	Keep Your Hands To Yourself	Georgia Satellites
3/14	1	2	39.	Somewhere Out There	Linda Ronstadt & James Ingram
3/21	1	2	40.	Let's Wait Awhile	Janet Jackson

TOP 40 HITS
1988

PK DATE	PK WKS	PK POS	RANK	TITLE	ARTIST
7/30	4	1	1.	Roll With It	Steve Winwood
12/24	3	1	2.	Every Rose Has Its Thorn	Poison
5/28	3	1	3.	One More Try	George Michael
12/10	2	1	4.	Look Away	Chicago
3/12	2	1	5.	Never Gonna Give You Up	Rick Astley
9/10	2	1	6.	Sweet Child O' Mine	Guns N' Roses
5/14	2	1	7.	Anything For You	Gloria Estefan & Miami Sound Machine
4/09	2	1	8.	Get Outta My Dreams, Get Into My Car	Billy Ocean
3/26	2	1	9.	Man In The Mirror	Michael Jackson
7/09	2	1	10.	The Flame	Cheap Trick
2/06	2	1	11.	Could've Been	Tiffany
9/24	2	1	12.	Don't Worry Be Happy	Bobby McFerrin
10/22	2	1	13.	Groovy Kind Of Love	Phil Collins
4/23	2	1	14.	Where Do Broken Hearts Go	Whitney Houston
2/27	2	1	15.	Father Figure	George Michael
11/19	2	1	16.	Bad Medicine	Bon Jovi
8/27	2	1	17.	Monkey	George Michael
1/30	1	1	18.	Need You Tonight	INXS
1/16	1	1	19.	Got My Mind Set On You	George Harrison
1/09	1	1	20.	So Emotional	Whitney Houston
11/12	1	1	21.	Wild, Wild West	The Escape Club
2/20	1	1	22.	Seasons Change	Expose
5/07	1	1	23.	Wishing Well	Terence Trent D'Arby
12/03	1	1	24.	Baby, I Love Your Way/Freebird Medley (Free Baby)	Will To Power
7/23	1	1	25.	Hold On To The Nights	Richard Marx
6/25	1	1	26.	Foolish Beat	Debbie Gibson
10/08	1	1	27.	Love Bites	Def Leppard
1/23	1	1	28.	The Way You Make Me Feel	Michael Jackson
10/15	1	1	29.	Red Red Wine	UB40
6/18	1	1	30.	Together Forever	Rick Astley
11/05	1	1	31.	Kokomo	The Beach Boys
7/02	1	1	32.	Dirty Diana	Michael Jackson
5/14	3	2	33.	Shattered Dreams	Johnny Hates Jazz
8/06	2	2	34.	Hands To Heaven	Breathe
3/26	2	2	35.	Endless Summer Nights	Richard Marx
9/10	2	2	36.	Simply Irresistible	Robert Palmer
2/20	2	2	37.	What Have I Done To Deserve This?	Pet Shop Boys/Dusty Springfield
4/16	2	2	38.	Devil Inside	INXS
7/09	2	2	39.	Mercedes Boy	Pebbles
7/23	1	2	40.	Pour Some Sugar On Me	Def Leppard

TOP 40 HITS
1989

PK DATE	PK WKS	PK POS	RANK	TITLE	ARTIST
12/23	4	1	1.	Another Day In Paradise	Phil Collins
10/07	4	1	2.	Miss You Much	Janet Jackson
2/11	3	1	3.	Straight Up	Paula Abdul
8/12	3	1	4.	Right Here Waiting	Richard Marx
3/04	3	1	5.	Lost In Your Eyes	Debbie Gibson
4/22	3	1	6.	Like A Prayer	Madonna
12/09	2	1	7.	We Didn't Start The Fire	Billy Joel
1/21	2	1	8.	Two Hearts	Phil Collins
11/11	2	1	9.	When I See You Smile	Bad English
11/25	2	1	10.	Blame It On The Rain	Milli Vanilli
5/20	2	1	11.	Forever Your Girl	Paula Abdul
9/23	2	1	12.	Girl I'm Gonna Miss You	Milli Vanilli
7/22	2	1	13.	Toy Soldiers	Martika
9/02	1	1	14.	Cold Hearted	Paula Abdul
9/16	1	1	15.	Don't Wanna Lose You	Gloria Estefan
6/10	1	1	16.	Wind Beneath My Wings	Bette Midler
1/14	1	1	17.	My Prerogative	Bobby Brown
4/15	1	1	18.	She Drives Me Crazy	Fine Young Cannibals
4/08	1	1	19.	The Look	Roxette
7/15	1	1	20.	If You Don't Know Me By Now	Simply Red
11/04	1	1	21.	Listen To Your Heart	Roxette
6/17	1	1	22.	I'll Be Loving You (Forever)	New Kids On The Block
7/01	1	1	23.	Baby Don't Forget My Number	Milli Vanilli
3/25	1	1	24.	The Living Years	Mike & The Mechanics
4/01	1	1	25.	Eternal Flame	Bangles
5/13	1	1	26.	I'll Be There For You	Bon Jovi
7/08	1	1	27.	Good Thing	Fine Young Cannibals
9/09	1	1	28.	Hangin' Tough	New Kids On The Block
8/05	1	1	29.	Batdance	Prince
2/04	1	1	30.	When I'm With You	Sheriff
6/03	1	1	31.	Rock On	Michael Damian
6/24	1	1	32.	Satisfied	Richard Marx
8/05	3	2	33.	On Our Own	Bobby Brown
12/23	2	2	34.	Don't Know Much	Linda Ronstadt feat. Aaron Neville
9/23	2	2	35.	Heaven	Warrant
5/20	2	2	36.	Real Love	Jody Watley
10/07	2	2	37.	Cherish	Madonna
7/15	2	2	38.	Express Yourself	Madonna
1/21	1	2	39.	Don't Rush Me	Taylor Dayne
4/01	1	2	40.	Girl You Know It's True	Milli Vanilli

TOP 40 HITS
1990

PK DATE	PK WKS	PK POS	RANK	TITLE	ARTIST
4/21	4	1	1.	Nothing Compares 2 U	Sinead O'Connor
8/04	4	1	2.	Vision Of Love	Mariah Carey
5/19	3	1	3.	Vogue	Madonna
3/03	3	1	4.	Escapade	Janet Jackson
2/10	3	1	5.	Opposites Attract	Paula Abdul with The Wild Pair
6/30	3	1	6.	Step By Step	New Kids On The Block
1/20	3	1	7.	How Am I Supposed To Live Without You	Michael Bolton
6/16	2	1	8.	It Must Have Been Love	Roxette
3/24	2	1	9.	Black Velvet	Alannah Myles
9/15	2	1	10.	Release Me	Wilson Phillips
7/21	2	1	11.	She Ain't Worth It	Glenn Medeiros/Bobby Brown
6/09	1	1	12.	Hold On	Wilson Phillips
9/08	1	1	13.	Blaze Of Glory	Jon Bon Jovi
9/01	1	1	14.	If Wishes Came True	Sweet Sensation
4/07	1	1	15.	Love Will Lead You Back	Taylor Dayne
4/14	1	1	16.	I'll Be Your Everything	Tommy Page
4/14	3	2	17.	Don't Wanna Fall In Love	Jane Child
1/20	2	2	18.	Pump Up The Jam	Technotronic Featuring Felly
5/26	2	2	19.	All I Wanna Do Is Make Love To You	Heart
2/10	2	2	20.	Two To Make It Right	Seduction
1/06	2	2	21.	Rhythm Nation	Janet Jackson
3/03	2	2	22.	Dangerous	Roxette
8/18	2	2	23.	Come Back To Me	Janet Jackson
8/04	1	2	24.	Cradle Of Love	Billy Idol
7/21	1	2	25.	Hold On	En Vogue
8/11	1	2	26.	The Power	Snap!
5/05	1	2	27.	I Wanna Be Rich	Calloway
6/09	4	3	28.	Poison	Bell Biv DeVoe
9/08	3	3	29.	Do Me!	Bell Biv DeVoe
4/21	3	3	30.	All Around The World	Lisa Stansfield
1/27	3	3	31.	Downtown Train	Rod Stewart
8/04	2	3	32.	Rub You The Right Way	Johnny Gill
3/10	2	3	33.	Roam	The B-52's
9/01	1	3	34.	Unskinny Bop	Poison
5/05	1	3	35.	How Can We Be Lovers	Michael Bolton
3/31	1	3	36.	I Wish It Would Rain Down	Phil Collins
1/20	2	4	37.	Everything	Jody Watley
6/02	1	4	38.	Alright	Janet Jackson
9/15	1	4	39.	Have You Seen Her	M.C. Hammer
6/30	1	4	40.	Do You Remember?	Phil Collins

Note The above ranking includes only those records that peaked on or before the 9/22/90 "Hot 100" chart.

THE TOP 100 ALBUMS

This section depicts, in rank order, the biggest No. 1 albums from March 24, 1956 through November 10, 1990. Prior to March 24, 1956, Billboard's Pop Albums charts were published sporadically — often 3 weeks between charts. It wasn't until March 24, 1956 that the albums charts were published on a regular weekly basis. The first No. 1 album on this new *Best Selling Pop Albums* chart was "Belafonte" by Harry Belafonte (No. 1 for 6 weeks), preceding Elvis Presley's debut album which hit No. 1 on May 5, 1956.

This ranking is based on the most weeks an album held the No. 1 position. Ties are broken according to this order: total weeks in the Top 10, total weeks in the Top 40, and finally, total weeks charted. The total weeks at No. 1 and total weeks in the Top 10 are shown below each album cover photo, along with the year the album peaked.

* - Album still in the Top 10 as of the November 10, 1990 cut-off date.

1. **"West Side Story"**
Soundtrack

#1 – 54 Weeks
Top 10 Weeks: 106
Year: 1962

2. **"Thriller"**
Michael Jackson

#1 – 37 Weeks
Top 10 Weeks: 78
Year: 1983

3. **"South Pacific"**
Soundtrack

#1 – 31 Weeks
Top 10 Weeks: 90
Year: 1958

4. **"Calypso"**
Harry Belafonte

#1 – 31 Weeks
Top 10 Weeks: 58
Year: 1956

5. **"Rumours"**
Fleetwood Mac

#1 – 31 Weeks
Top 10 Weeks: 52
Year: 1977

6. **"Saturday Night Fever"**
Bee Gees/Soundtrack

#1 – 24 Weeks
Top 10 Weeks: 35
Year: 1978

7. **"Purple Rain"**
Prince And The Revolution/Soundtrack

#1 – 24 Weeks
Top 10 Weeks: 32
Year: 1984

8. **"Please Hammer Don't Hurt 'Em"**
M.C. Hammer

#1 – 21 Weeks
Top 10 Weeks: 31*
Year: 1990

9. **"Blue Hawaii"**
Elvis Presley/Soundtrack

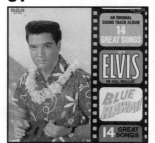

#1 – 20 Weeks
Top 10 Weeks: 39
Year: 1961

10. **"Dirty Dancing"**
Soundtrack

#1 – 18 Weeks
Top 10 Weeks: 48
Year: 1987

11. **"More Of The Monkees"**
The Monkees

#1 – 18 Weeks
Top 10 Weeks: 25
Year: 1967

12. **"Synchronicity"**
The Police

#1 – 17 Weeks
Top 10 Weeks: 40
Year: 1983

13. **"The Sound Of Music"**
Original Cast

#1 – 16 Weeks
Top 10 Weeks: 105
Year: 1960

14. **"Days Of Wine And Roses"**
Andy Williams

#1 – 16 Weeks
Top 10 Weeks: 23
Year: 1963

15.
"My Fair Lady"
Original Cast

#1 – 15 Weeks
Top 10 Weeks: 173
Year: 1956

16.
"Tapestry"
Carole King

#1 – 15 Weeks
Top 10 Weeks: 46
Year: 1971

17.
"Sgt. Pepper's Lonely Hearts Club Band"
The Beatles

#1 – 15 Weeks
Top 10 Weeks: 33
Year: 1967

18.
"Business As Usual"
Men At Work

#1 – 15 Weeks
Top 10 Weeks: 31
Year: 1982

19.
"The Kingston Trio At Large"
The Kingston Trio

#1 – 15 Weeks
Top 10 Weeks: 31
Year: 1959

20.
"Hi Infidelity"
REO Speedwagon

#1 – 15 Weeks
Top 10 Weeks: 30
Year: 1981

21.
"The Wall"
Pink Floyd

#1 – 15 Weeks
Top 10 Weeks: 27
Year: 1980

22. **"Mary Poppins"**
Soundtrack

#1 – 14 Weeks
Top 10 Weeks: 48
Year: 1965

23. **"Whitney Houston"**
Whitney Houston

#1 – 14 Weeks
Top 10 Weeks: 46
Year: 1986

24. **"The Button-Down Mind Of Bob Newhart"**
Bob Newhart

#1 – 14 Weeks
Top 10 Weeks: 44
Year: 1960

25. **"Exodus"**
Soundtrack

#1 – 14 Weeks
Top 10 Weeks: 38
Year: 1961

26. **"Songs In The Key Of Life"**
Stevie Wonder

#1 – 14 Weeks
Top 10 Weeks: 35
Year: 1976

27. **"Modern Sounds In Country And Western Music"**
Ray Charles

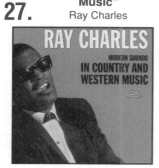

#1 – 14 Weeks
Top 10 Weeks: 33
Year: 1962

28. **"A Hard Day's Night"**
The Beatles/Soundtrack

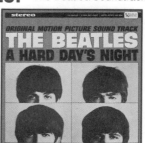

#1 – 14 Weeks
Top 10 Weeks: 28
Year: 1964

29. "Persuasive Percussion"
Enoch Light/Terry Snyder and The All Stars

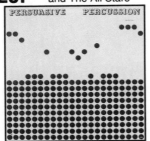

#1 – 13 Weeks
Top 10 Weeks: 43
Year: 1960

30. "Judy At Carnegie Hall"
Judy Garland

#1 – 13 Weeks
Top 10 Weeks: 37
Year: 1961

31. "The Monkees"
The Monkees

#1 – 13 Weeks
Top 10 Weeks: 32
Year: 1966

32. "Hair"
Original Cast

#1 – 13 Weeks
Top 10 Weeks: 28
Year: 1969

33. "The Music Man"
Original Cast

#1 – 12 Weeks
Top 10 Weeks: 63
Year: 1958

34. "Faith"
George Michael

#1 – 12 Weeks
Top 10 Weeks: 51
Year: 1988

35. "Breakfast At Tiffany's"
Henry Mancini/Soundtrack

#1 – 12 Weeks
Top 10 Weeks: 46
Year: 1962

36. **"Sold Out"**
The Kingston Trio

#1 – 12 Weeks
Top 10 Weeks: 29
Year: 1960

37. **"Grease"**
Olivia Newton-John/
Soundtrack

#1 – 12 Weeks
Top 10 Weeks: 29
Year: 1978

38. **"The First Family"**
Vaughn Meader

#1 – 12 Weeks
Top 10 Weeks: 17
Year: 1962

39. **"Calcutta!"**
Lawrence Welk

#1 – 11 Weeks
Top 10 Weeks: 33
Year: 1961

40. **"Whitney"**
Whitney Houston

#1 – 11 Weeks
Top 10 Weeks: 31
Year: 1987

41. **"Abbey Road"**
The Beatles

#1 – 11 Weeks
Top 10 Weeks: 27
Year: 1969

42. **"Meet The Beatles!"**
The Beatles

#1 – 11 Weeks
Top 10 Weeks: 21
Year: 1964

43.
"Miami Vice"
TV Soundtrack

#1 – 11 Weeks
Top 10 Weeks: 18
Year: 1985

44.
"Forever Your Girl"
Paula Abdul

#1 – 10 Weeks
Top 10 Weeks: 64
Year: 1989

45.
"Around The World In 80 Days"
Soundtrack

#1 – 10 Weeks
Top 10 Weeks: 54
Year: 1957

46.
"Gigi"
Soundtrack

#1 – 10 Weeks
Top 10 Weeks: 54
Year: 1958

47.
"Frampton Comes Alive!"
Peter Frampton

#1 – 10 Weeks
Top 10 Weeks: 52
Year: 1976

48.
"Elvis Presley"
Elvis Presley

#1 – 10 Weeks
Top 10 Weeks: 43
Year: 1956

49.
"The Music From Peter Gunn"
Henry Mancini

#1 – 10 Weeks
Top 10 Weeks: 43
Year: 1959

50. **"4"**
Foreigner

#1 – 10 Weeks
Top 10 Weeks: 34
Year: 1981

51. **"G.I. Blues"**
Elvis Presley/Soundtrack

#1 – 10 Weeks
Top 10 Weeks: 29
Year: 1960

52. **"Footloose"**
Soundtrack

#1 – 10 Weeks
Top 10 Weeks: 20
Year: 1984

53. **"String Along"**
The Kingston Trio

#1 – 10 Weeks
Top 10 Weeks: 20
Year: 1960

54. **"Loving You"**
Elvis Presley/Soundtrack

#1 – 10 Weeks
Top 10 Weeks: 19
Year: 1957

55. **"The Singing Nun"**
The Singing Nun

#1 – 10 Weeks
Top 10 Weeks: 18
Year: 1963

56. **"Bridge Over
Troubled Water"**
Simon and Garfunkel

#1 – 10 Weeks
Top 10 Weeks: 17
Year: 1970

85

57.
**"Elton John –
Greatest Hits"**
Elton John

#1 – 10 Weeks
Top 10 Weeks: 11
Year: 1974

58.
"Brothers In Arms"
Dire Straits

#1 – 9 Weeks
Top 10 Weeks: 37
Year: 1985

59.
"The Joshua Tree"
U2

#1 – 9 Weeks
Top 10 Weeks: 36
Year: 1987

60.
"What Now My Love"
Herb Alpert & The Tijuana
Brass

#1 – 9 Weeks
Top 10 Weeks: 32
Year: 1966

61.
"Asia"
Asia

#1 – 9 Weeks
Top 10 Weeks: 27
Year: 1982

62.
"The Graduate"
Simon & Garfunkel/
Soundtrack

#1 – 9 Weeks
Top 10 Weeks: 26
Year: 1968

63.
"American Fool"
John Cougar

#1 – 9 Weeks
Top 10 Weeks: 22
Year: 1982

64. ### "Tattoo You"
The Rolling Stones

#1 – 9 Weeks
Top 10 Weeks: 22
Year: 1981

65. ### "Stars For A Summer Night"
Various Artists

#1 – 9 Weeks
Top 10 Weeks: 21
Year: 1961

66. ### "The Long Run"
Eagles

#1 – 9 Weeks
Top 10 Weeks: 21
Year: 1979

67. ### "Nice 'N' Easy"
Frank Sinatra

#1 – 9 Weeks
Top 10 Weeks: 19
Year: 1960

68. ### "Cosmo's Factory"
Creedence Clearwater Revival

#1 – 9 Weeks
Top 10 Weeks: 19
Year: 1970

69. ### "Beatles '65"
The Beatles

#1 – 9 Weeks
Top 10 Weeks: 16
Year: 1965

70. ### "Help!"
The Beatles/Soundtrack

#1 – 9 Weeks
Top 10 Weeks: 15
Year: 1965

71.
"The Beatles [White Album]"
The Beatles

#1 – 9 Weeks
Top 10 Weeks: 15
Year: 1968

72.
"Pearl"
Janis Joplin

#1 – 9 Weeks
Top 10 Weeks: 15
Year: 1971

73.
"Chicago V"
Chicago

#1 – 9 Weeks
Top 10 Weeks: 13
Year: 1972

74.
"Whipped Cream & Other Delights"
Herb Alpert's Tijuana Brass

#1 – 8 Weeks
Top 10 Weeks: 61
Year: 1965

75.
"Sing Along With Mitch"
Mitchel Miller & The Gang

#1 – 8 Weeks
Top 10 Weeks: 53
Year: 1958

76.
"Slippery When Wet"
Bon Jovi

#1 – 8 Weeks
Top 10 Weeks: 46
Year: 1986

77.
"Girl You Know It's True"
Milli Vanilli

#1 – 8 Weeks
Top 10 Weeks: 41
Year: 1989

78.
"Goodbye Yellow Brick Road"
Elton John

#1 – 8 Weeks
Top 10 Weeks: 36
Year: 1973

79.
"Love Is The Thing"
Nat "King" Cole

#1 – 8 Weeks
Top 10 Weeks: 31
Year: 1957

80.
"Hotel California"
Eagles

#1 – 8 Weeks
Top 10 Weeks: 28
Year: 1977

81.
"Here We Go Again!"
The Kingston Trio

#1 – 8 Weeks
Top 10 Weeks: 26
Year: 1959

82.
"Double Fantasy"
John Lennon/Yoko Ono

#1 – 8 Weeks
Top 10 Weeks: 24
Year: 1980

83.
"52nd Street"
Billy Joel

#1 – 8 Weeks
Top 10 Weeks: 22
Year: 1978

84.
"Cheap Thrills"
Big Brother And The Holding Company

#1 – 8 Weeks
Top 10 Weeks: 19
Year: 1968

85.
"Magical Mystery Tour"
The Beatles

#1 – 8 Weeks
Top 10 Weeks: 14
Year: 1968

86.
"My Son, The Nut"
Allan Sherman

#1 – 8 Weeks
Top 10 Weeks: 12
Year: 1963

87.
"Peter, Paul And Mary"
Peter, Paul and Mary

#1 – 7 Weeks
Top 10 Weeks: 85
Year: 1962

88.
"Born In The U.S.A."
Bruce Springsteen

#1 – 7 Weeks
Top 10 Weeks: 83
Year: 1984

89.
"Blood, Sweat & Tears"
Blood, Sweat & Tears

#1 – 7 Weeks
Top 10 Weeks: 50
Year: 1969

90.
"Stereo 35/MM"
Enoch Light & The Light Brigade

#1 – 7 Weeks
Top 10 Weeks: 42
Year: 1961

91.
"Tchaikovsky: Piano Concerto No. 1"
Van Cliburn

#1 – 7 Weeks
Top 10 Weeks: 39
Year: 1958

92.
"No Jacket Required"
Phil Collins

#1 – 7 Weeks
Top 10 Weeks: 31
Year: 1985

93.
"The Raw & The Cooked"
Fine Young Cannibals

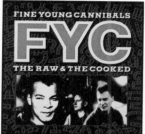

#1 – 7 Weeks
Top 10 Weeks: 27
Year: 1989

94.
"Led Zeppelin II"
Led Zeppelin

#1 – 7 Weeks
Top 10 Weeks: 24
Year: 1969

95.
"Wings At The Speed Of Sound"
Wings

#1 – 7 Weeks
Top 10 Weeks: 21
Year: 1976

96.
"Bookends"
Simon & Garfunkel

#1 – 7 Weeks
Top 10 Weeks: 20
Year: 1968

97.
"Licensed To Ill"
Beastie Boys

#1 – 7 Weeks
Top 10 Weeks: 19
Year: 1987

98.
"In Through The Out Door"
Led Zeppelin

#1 – 7 Weeks
Top 10 Weeks: 18
Year: 1979

99.
"American Pie"
Don McLean

#1 – 7 Weeks
Top 10 Weeks: 17
Year: 1972

100.
"Captain Fantastic And The Brown Dirt Cowboy"
Elton John

#1 – 7 Weeks
Top 10 Weeks: 17
Year: 1975

Their distinctive new sound has already caught on !

THE
MOODY BLUES

NIGHTS
IN
WHITE
SATIN

Produced by Tony Clarke

DERAM
A PRODUCT OF
LONDON
85023

THE ARTISTS

This section lists, alphabetically by artist name, every single listed in the *Top 1000* ranking.

Each artist's hits are listed in rank order, showing the *Top 1000* ranking next to each title, along the original label and number. Because the artist's hits are listed in rank order, it makes for a handy guide to easily see each artist's all-time greatest hits.

A

ABBA
567 Dancing Queen ....Atlantic 3372
ABBOTT, Gregory
563 Shake You Down ....Columbia 06191
ABDUL, Paula
245 Straight Up ....Virgin 99256
249 Opposites Attract................Virgin 99158
    Paula Abdul With The Wild Pair
443 Forever Your Girl ....Virgin 99230
570 Cold Hearted ....Virgin 99196
ADAMS, Bryan
451 Heaven ....A&M 2729
A-HA
605 Take On Me ....Warner 29011
AIR SUPPLY
584 The One That You Love ....Arista 0604
801 All Out Of Love..................Arista 0520
836 Making Love Out Of Nothing At
    All....................................Arista 9056
ALPERT, Herb
153 This Guy's In Love With You ......A&M 929
326 Rise ....A&M 2151
AMERICA
197 A Horse With No Name ....Warner 7555
781 Sister Golden Hair ....Warner 8086
ANDERSON, Carl - see LORING, Gloria
ANGELS, The
212 My Boyfriend's Back ....Smash 1834
ANIMALS, The
244 The House Of The Rising Sun ...MGM 13264
ANKA, Paul
120 Lonely Boy ....ABC-Para. 10022
278 (You're) Having My Baby.....United Art. 454
500 Diana ....ABC-Para. 9831
828 Put Your Head On My
    Shoulder......................ABC-Para. 10040
955 Puppy Love ....ABC-Para. 10082
ARCHIES, The
102 Sugar, Sugar ....Calendar 1008
ARMSTRONG, Louis
496 Hello, Dolly! ....Kapp 573
ASSOCIATION, The
136 Windy...............................Warner 7041
276 Cherish.............................Valiant 747
928 Never My Love...................Warner 7074
ASTLEY, Rick
401 Never Gonna Give You Up ....RCA 5347
731 Together Forever ....RCA 8319
ATLANTIC STARR
616 Always ....Warner 28455
AUSTIN, Patti, with James Ingram
313 Baby, Come To Me..............Qwest 50036
AVALON, Frankie
74 Venus ....Chancellor 1031
554 Why ....Chancellor 1045
AWB (Average White Band)
644 Pick Up The Pieces..............Atlantic 3229

94

B

BACHMAN-TURNER OVERDRIVE
765 You Ain't Seen Nothing Yet ..Mercury 73622
BAD ENGLISH
439 When I See You Smile ....Epic 69082
BAILEY, Philip, with Phil Collins
932 Easy Lover ....Columbia 04679
BANANARAMA
650 Venus ....London 886056
BANGLES
145 Walk Like An Egyptian ....Columbia 06257
707 Eternal Flame.................Columbia 68533
BASIL, Toni
512 Mickey ....Chrysalis 2638
BAXTER, Les
32 The Poor People Of Paris........Capitol 3336
BAY CITY ROLLERS
732 Saturday Night ....Arista 0149
BEACH BOYS, The
339 I Get Around.......................Capitol 5174
424 Help Me, Rhonda ....Capitol 5395
662 Good Vibrations...................Capitol 5676
754 Kokomo ....Elektra 69385
BEATLES, The
8 Hey Jude...........................Apple 2276
26 I Want To Hold Your Hand .....Capitol 5112
85 Get Back...........................Apple 2490
88 Can't Buy Me Love ....Capitol 5150
160 Yesterday..........................Capitol 5498
243 Hello Goodbye ....Capitol 2056
268 We Can Work It Out ....Capitol 5555
270 I Feel Fine ....Capitol 5327
277 Help! ....Capitol 5476
299 She Loves You ....Swan 4152
300 Let It Be ....Apple 2764
388 A Hard Day's Night ....Capitol 5222
481 The Long And Winding Road ....Apple 2832
489 Paperback Writer ....Capitol 5651
490 Eight Days A Week.............Capitol 5371
538 Come Together ....Apple 2654
682 All You Need Is Love............Capitol 5964
745 Love Me Do ....Tollie 9008
752 Ticket To Ride ....Capitol 5407
777 Penny Lane........................Capitol 5810
812 Twist And Shout...................Tollie 9001
BEE GEES
16 Night Fever ....RSO 889
95 Stayin' Alive ....RSO 885
121 How Can You Mend A Broken
    Heart...............................Atco 6824
163 How Deep Is Your Love ....RSO 882
322 Too Much Heaven ....RSO 913
333 Tragedy ....RSO 918
383 Jive Talkin' ....RSO 510
649 You Should Be Dancing.............RSO 853
762 Love You Inside Out ....RSO 925
BELL, Archie, & The Drells
344 Tighten Up ....Atlantic 2478

BELLAMY BROTHERS
651 Let Your Love Flow ....Warner 8169
BENTON, Brook
850 The Boll Weevil Song ....Mercury 71820
BERLIN
633 Take My Breath Away.......Columbia 05903
BERRY, Chuck
471 My Ding-A-Ling ....Chess 2131
860 Sweet Little Sixteen ....Chess 1683
BILK, Mr. Acker
509 Stranger On The Shore...........Atco 6217
BLONDIE
44 Call Me...........................Chrysalis 2414
374 Rapture ....Chrysalis 2485
513 The Tide Is High................Chrysalis 2465
617 Heart Of Glass.................Chrysalis 2295
BLOOD, SWEAT & TEARS
859 Spinning Wheel ....Columbia 44871
876 You've Made Me So Very
        Happy ....Columbia 44776
BLUE SWEDE
629 Hooked On A Feeling ....EMI 3627
BOLTON, Michael
273 How Am I Supposed To Live Without
        You ....Columbia 73017
BONDS, Gary U.S.
386 Quarter To Three ....Legrand 1008
BON JOVI
157 Livin' On A Prayer ....Mercury 888184
465 Bad Medicine..................Mercury 870657
695 You Give Love A Bad
        Name.....................Mercury 884953
711 I'll Be There For You.........Mercury 872564
BON JOVI, Jon
585 Blaze Of Glory ....Mercury 875896
BOONE, Debby
4 You Light Up My Life...........Warner 8455
BOONE, Pat
18 Love Letters In The Sand ....Dot 15570
38 April Love ....Dot 15660
92 I Almost Lost My Mind ....Dot 15472
282 Ain't That A Shame ....Dot 15377
497 Don't Forbid Me ....Dot 15521
739 Moody River ....Dot 16209
BOSTON
468 Amanda ....MCA 52756
BOWIE, David
446 Fame ....RCA 10320
519 Let's Dance ....EMI America 8158
BOX TOPS, The
150 The Letter ....Mala 565
979 Cry Like A Baby.....................Mala 593
BRANIGAN, Laura
829 Gloria...............................Atlantic 4048
BREAD
523 Make It With You ....Elektra 45686
BREATHE
963 Hands To Heaven..................A&M 2991

BROTHERS FOUR, The
806 Greenfields.....................Columbia 41571
BROWN, Bobby
407 She Ain't Worth It.................MCA 53831
        Glenn Medeiros Featuring Bobby Brown
606 My Prerogative....................MCA 53383
867 On Our Own ....MCA 53662
BROWNS, The
119 The Three Bells ....RCA 7555
B.T. EXPRESS
939 Do It ('Til You're Satisfied) .Roadshow 12395
BUCKINGHAMS, The
433 Kind Of A Drag ...................U.S.A. 860
BYRDS, The
238 Turn! Turn! Turn! (To Everything There Is
        A Season).....................Columbia 43424
677 Mr. Tambourine Man ....Columbia 43271

C

CAMPBELL, Glen
316 Rhinestone Cowboy..............Capitol 4095
572 Southern Nights ....Capitol 4376
CAPTAIN & TENNILLE
158 Love Will Keep Us Together ......A&M 1672
492 Do That To Me One More
        Time....................Casablanca 2215
CARA, Irene
37 Flashdance...What A
        Feeling...................Casablanca 811440
CAREY, Mariah
155 Vision Of Love ....Columbia 73348
CARLISLE, Belinda
691 Heaven Is A Place On Earth .....MCA 53181
CARMEN, Eric
866 All By Myself ....Arista 0165
CARNES, Kim
7 Bette Davis Eyes ....EMI America 8077
CARPENTERS
109 (They Long To Be) Close To
        You ....A&M 1183
361 Top Of The World ....A&M 1468
766 Please Mr. Postman ....A&M 1646
807 We've Only Just Begun...........A&M 1217
925 Superstar.........................A&M 1289
958 Rainy Days And Mondays........A&M 1260
988 Hurting Each Other................A&M 1322
CASH, Johnny
861 A Boy Named Sue ....Columbia 44944
CASSIDY, Shaun
648 Da Doo Ron Ron ....Warner 8365
CETERA, Peter
445 Glory Of Love ....Full Moon 28662
693 The Next Time I Fall.........Full Moon 28597
        Peter Cetera w/Amy Grant
CHAMPS, The
64 Tequila ....Challenge 1016
CHANDLER, Gene
237 Duke Of Earl ....Vee-Jay 416

CHANNEL, Bruce
235 Hey! Baby..........................Smash 1731

CHAPIN, Harry
730 Cat's In The Cradle..............Elektra 45203

CHARLES, Ray
68 I Can't Stop Loving You.....ABC-Para. 10330
390 Hit The Road Jack...........ABC-Para. 10244
772 Georgia On My Mind........ABC-Para. 10135

CHEAP TRICK
441 The Flame..........................Epic 07745

CHECKER, Chubby
161 The Twist..........................Parkway 811
221 Pony Time........................Parkway 818
887 Limbo Rock.....................Parkway 849

CHER
Also see Sonny & Cher.
332 Gypsys, Tramps & Thieves........Kapp 2146
373 Half-Breed.........................MCA 40102
737 Dark Lady..........................MCA 40161

CHIC
34 Le Freak.........................Atlantic 3519
548 Good Times.....................Atlantic 3584

CHICAGO
289 Hard To Say I'm Sorry.......Full Moon 29979
321 If You Leave Me Now........Columbia 10390
358 Look Away.......................Reprise 27766

CHIFFONS, The
139 He's So Fine.....................Laurie 3152

CHILD, Jane
865 Don't Wanna Fall In Love......Warner 19933

CHI-LITES, The
631 Oh Girl............................Brunswick 55471

CHIPMUNKS with David Seville
159 The Chipmunk Song............Liberty 55168

CHORDETTES, The
949 Lollipop...........................Cadence 1345

CHRISTIE, Lou
748 Lightnin' Strikes...................MGM 13412

CLAPTON, Eric
771 I Shot The Sheriff.....................RSO 409

CLARK, Dave, Five
747 Over And Over.......................Epic 9863

CLARK, Petula
341 Downtown.........................Warner 5494
483 My Love............................Warner 5684

CLUB NOUVEAU
470 Lean On Me.....................Warner 28430

COASTERS, The
544 Yakety Yak........................Atco 6116
851 Charlie Brown......................Atco 6132

COCKER, Joe, and Jennifer Warnes
247 Up Where We Belong...........Island 99996

COLE, Nat 'King'
920 Ramblin' Rose....................Capitol 4804

COLLINS, Phil
118 Another Day In Paradise.....Atlantic 88774
187 Against All Odds (Take A Look At Me
Now)...........................Atlantic 89700

411 Two Hearts......................Atlantic 88980
455 Groovy Kind Of Love...........Atlantic 89017
467 One More Night.................Atlantic 89588
534 Separate Lives.................Atlantic 89498
Phil Collins And Marilyn Martin
709 Sussudio.........................Atlantic 89560
932 Easy Lover.....................Columbia 04679
Philip Bailey With Phil Collins

COMMODORES
292 Three Times A Lady............Motown 1443
499 Still.............................Motown 1474

COMO, Perry
283 Round And Round.................RCA 6815
493 Hot Diggity (Dog Ziggity Boom)..RCA 6427
503 Catch A Falling Star.............RCA 7128

CONTI, Bill
587 Gonna Fly Now.................United Art. 940

COOKE, Sam
169 You Send Me.....................Keen 34013
918 Chain Gang.......................RCA 7783

CORNELIUS BROTHERS & SISTER ROSE
927 Too Late To Turn Back
Now..........................United Art. 50910

CORTEZ, Dave 'Baby'
628 The Happy Organ.................Clock 1009

COUGAR, John
114 Jack & Diane......................Riva 210
796 Hurts So Good....................Riva 209

COWSILLS, The
921 Hair..............................MGM 14026
923 The Rain, The Park & Other
Things........................MGM 13810

CRAMER, Floyd
802 Last Date.........................RCA 7775

CREEDENCE CLEARWATER REVIVAL
857 Proud Mary.......................Fantasy 619

CRESTS, The
913 16 Candles.........................Coed 506

CRICKETS, The
533 That'll Be The Day...........Brunswick 55009

CROCE, Jim
359 Bad, Bad Leroy Brown............ABC 11359
418 Time In A Bottle...................ABC 11405

CROSS, Christopher
172 Arthur's Theme (Best That You Can
Do)............................Warner 49787
634 Sailing...........................Warner 49507
804 Ride Like The Wind.............Warner 49184

CRYSTALS, The
416 He's A Rebel.......................Philles 106

CULTURE CLUB
200 Karma Chameleon................Virgin 04221
835 Do You Really Want To Hurt
Me..............................Epic 03368
903 Time (Clock Of The Heart)........Epic 03796

CUTTING CREW
460 (I Just) Died In Your Arms......Virgin 99481

D

DALE & GRACE
420   I'm Leaving It Up To You........Montel 921
DAMIAN, Michael
760   Rock On ....Cypress 1420
DANNY & THE JUNIORS
22   At The Hop ....ABC-Para. 9871
D'ARBY, Terence Trent
688   Wishing Well ....Columbia 07675
DARIN, Bobby
5   Mack The Knife.....................Atco 6147
DAVIS, Mac
206   Baby Don't Get Hooked On
    Me ....Columbia 45618
DAVIS, Sammy Jr.
246   The Candy Man...................MGM 14320
DAWN
107   Tie A Yellow Ribbon Round The Ole Oak
    Tree ....Bell 45318
180   Knock Three Times....................Bell 938
279   He Don't Love You (Like I Love
    You)............................Elektra 45240
    Tony Orlando & Dawn
DAY, Bobby
889   Rock-in Robin........................Class 229
DAY, Doris
820   Whatever Will Be, Will Be (Que Sera,
    Sera) ....Columbia 40704
DAYNE, Taylor
694   Love Will Lead You Back ....Arista 9938
DEAN, Jimmy
77   Big Bad John ....Columbia 42175
DEE, Joey, & the Starliters
181   Peppermint Twist - Part I ......Roulette 4401
DEE, Kiki - see JOHN, Elton
DEES, Rick, and His Cast Of Idiots
514   Disco Duck (Part 1) ....RSO 857
DEF LEPPARD
710   Love Bites.......................Mercury 870402
DENVER, John
423   Annie's Song ....RCA 0295
640   Sunshine On My Shoulders ....RCA 0213
755   Thank God I'm A Country Boy ..RCA 10239
779   I'm Sorry ....RCA 10353
817   Calypso ....RCA 10353
DeSARIO, Teri, with K.C.
933   Yes, I'm Ready ....Casablanca 2227
DEXYS MIDNIGHT RUNNERS
696   Come On Eileen ....Mercury 76189
DIAMOND, Neil
307   You Don't Bring Me
    Flowers.......................Columbia 10840
    Barbra Streisand & Neil Diamond
630   Cracklin' Rosie.......................Uni 55250
741   Song Sung Blue......................Uni 55326
831   Love On The Rocks ....Capitol 4939
DIAMONDS, The
786   Little Darlin' ....Mercury 71060

DINNING, Mark
308   Teen Angel ....MGM 12845
DION
349   Runaround Sue ....Laurie 3110
875   Ruby Baby ....Columbia 42662
DIRE STRAITS
226   Money For Nothing ....Warner 28950
DIXIE CUPS, The
267   Chapel Of Love...................Red Bird 001
DOGGETT, Bill
818   Honky Tonk (Parts 1 & 2)........King 4950
DOMINO, Fats
819   Blueberry Hill ....Imperial 5407
DONALDSON, Bo, And The Heywoods
415   Billy, Don't Be A Hero ....ABC 11435
DONOVAN
676   Sunshine Superman ....Epic 10045
864   Mellow Yellow ....Epic 10098
DOOBIE BROTHERS, The
547   What A Fool Believes ....Warner 8725
653   Black Water ....Warner 8062
DOORS, The
202   Light My Fire ....Elektra 45615
356   Hello, I Love You ....Elektra 45635
DORSEY, Jimmy
795   So Rare ....Fraternity 755
DOUGLAS, Carl
382   Kung Fu Fighting...........20th Century 2140
DOVELLS, The
902   Bristol Stomp ....Parkway 827
DOWELL, Joe
655   Wooden Heart ....Smash 1708
DRIFTERS, The
203   Save The Last Dance For Me...Atlantic 2071
DURAN DURAN
366   The Reflex...........................Capitol 5345
462   A View To A Kill.................Capitol 5475
810   The Wild Boys ....Capitol 5417

E

EAGLES
520   One Of These Nights ....Asylum 45257
552   Heartache Tonight ....Asylum 46545
574   Hotel California ....Asylum 45386
647   New Kid In Town ....Asylum 45373
706   Best Of My Love ....Asylum 45218
985   Lyin' Eyes........................Asylum 45279
EARTH, WIND & FIRE
756   Shining Star ....Columbia 10090
904   After The Love Has Gone........ARC 11033
EASTON, Sheena
440   Morning Train (Nine To
    Five) ....EMI America 8071
EDWARDS, Tommy
45   It's All In The Game ....MGM 12688
ELEGANTS, The
508   Little Star ....Apt 25005

GAYE, Marvin
29   I Heard It Through The
      Grapevine........................Tamla 54176
286 Let's Get It On..................Tamla 54234
541 Got To Give It Up (Pt. I)........Tamla 54280
849 What's Going On................Tamla 54201

GAYLE, Crystal
830 Don't It Make My Brown Eyes
      Blue ....United Art. 1016

GAYNOR, Gloria
168 I Will Survive ....Polydor 14508

GEILS, J., Band
43   Centerfold.....................EMI America 8102

GENESIS
733 Invisible Touch ....Atlantic 89407

GENTRY, Bobbie
137 Ode To Billie Joe ....Capitol 5950

GIBB, Andy
21   Shadow Dancing ....RSO 893
91   I Just Want To Be Your
      Everything ....RSO 872
290 (Love Is) Thicker Than Water.......RSO 883

GIBSON, Debbie
259 Lost In Your Eyes ....Atlantic 88970
705 Foolish Beat....................Atlantic 89109

GILDER, Nick
527 Hot Child In The City ....Chrysalis 2226

GILMER, Jimmy, and The Fireballs
78   Sugar Shack ....Dot 16487

GO-GO'S
839 We Got The Beat ..................I.R.S. 9903

GOLDSBORO, Bobby
79   Honey.........................United Art. 50283

GORE, Lesley
427 It's My Party ....Mercury 72119
884 You Don't Own Me ....Mercury 72206

GRACIE, Charlie
376 Butterfly............................Cameo 105

GRAND FUNK RAILROAD
447 The Loco-Motion ....Capitol 3840
720 We're An American Band ......Capitol 3660

GRANT, Amy - see CETERA, Peter

GRANT, Eddy
794 Electric Avenue ....Portrait 03793

GRANT, Gogi
12   The Wayward Wind.................Era 1013

GREEN, Al
543 Let's Stay Together ....Hi 2202

GREENE, Lorne
678 Ringo ....RCA 8444

GUESS WHO, The
224 American Woman ....RCA 0325

GUNS N' ROSES
402 Sweet Child O' Mine.............Geffen 27963

H

HALEY, Bill, and His Comets
11   Rock Around The Clock ....Decca 29124

HALL, Daryl, & John Oates
98   Maneater ....RCA 13354
213 Kiss On My List ....RCA 12142
319 Private Eyes......................RCA 12296
323 Out Of Touch ....RCA 13916
450 Rich Girl.........................RCA 10860
502 I Can't Go For That (No Can
      Do)............................RCA 12357
803 Say It Isn't So....................RCA 13654

HAMILTON, JOE FRANK & REYNOLDS
734 Fallin' In Love ....Playboy 6024

HAMMER, Jan
632 Miami Vice Theme.................MCA 52666

HARRISON, George
124 My Sweet Lord ....Apple 2995
569 Got My Mind Set On You ..Dark Horse 28178
673 Give Me Love - (Give Me Peace On
      Earth) ....Apple 1862
873 All Those Years Ago ....Dark Horse 49725

HARRISON, Wilbert
384 Kansas City..........................Fury 1023

HATHAWAY, Donny - see FLACK, Roberta

HAYES, Isaac
352 Theme From Shaft ....Enterprise 9038

HEART
216 Alone ....Capitol 44002
714 These Dreams ....Capitol 5541
917 All I Wanna Do Is Make Love To
      You ....Capitol 44507

HEATWAVE
896 Boogie Nights ....Epic 50370

HEBB, Bobby
982 Sunny ....Philips 40365

HERMAN'S HERMITS
269 Mrs. Brown You've Got A Lovely
      Daughter ....MGM 13341
753 I'm Henry VIII, I Am.............MGM 13367
981 Can't You Hear My Heartbeat ..MGM 13310

HEYWOOD, Eddie - see WINTERHALTER, Hugo

HIGHWAYMEN, The
354 Michael.........................United Art. 258

HOLLIES, The
922 Long Cool Woman (In A Black
      Dress) ....Epic 10871

HOLLY, Buddy - see CRICKETS, The

HOLLYWOOD ARGYLES
594 Alley-Oop ....Lute 5905

HOLMES, Clint
909 Playground In My Mind ....Epic 10891

HOLMES, Rupert
188 Escape (The Pina Colada
      Song) ....Infinity 50035

HONEY CONE, The
590 Want Ads......................Hot Wax 7011

HOPKIN, Mary
856 Those Were The Days ....Apple 1801

HORNSBY, Bruce, & The Range
568 The Way It Is ....RCA 5023

HORTON, Johnny
  41   The Battle Of New Orleans ..Columbia 41339
HOUSTON, Thelma
  561   Don't Leave Me This Way ......Tamla 54278
HOUSTON, Whitney
  252   Greatest Love Of All ....Arista 9466
  331   I Wanna Dance With Somebody (Who
        Loves Me)....................Arista 9598
  414   Didn't We Almost Have It All ...Arista 9616
  437   How Will I Know ....Arista 9434
  461   Where Do Broken Hearts Go ....Arista 9674
  583   So Emotional ....Arista 9642
  608   Saving All My Love For You .....Arista 9381
HUES CORPORATION, The
  769   Rock The Boat ....RCA 0232
HUMAN LEAGUE, The
  170   Don't You Want Me................A&M 2397
  610   Human ....A&M 2861
HUNTER, Tab
  42   Young Love ....Dot 15533
HYLAND, Brian
  592   Itsy Bitsy Teenie Weenie Yellow Polkadot
        Bikini................................Kapp 342

I

IDOL, Billy
  728   Mony Mony 'Live'..............Chrysalis 43161
IMPALAS, The
  952   Sorry (I Ran All the Way Home) ..Cub 9022
INGMANN, Jorgen, & His Guitar
  995   Apache...............................Atco 6184
INGRAM, James - see AUSTIN, Patti
INXS
  560   Need You Tonight ....Atlantic 89188
  997   Devil Inside ....Atlantic 89144

J

JACKS, Terry
  215   Seasons In The Sun ....Bell 45432
JACKSON, Janet
  148   Miss You Much ....A&M 1445
  217   Escapade ....A&M 1490
  459   When I Think Of You ....A&M 2855
  976   Rhythm Nation.....................A&M 1455
  1000 Come Back To Me ....A&M 1475
JACKSON, Michael
  28   Billie Jean ....Epic 03509
  40   Say Say Say ....Columbia 04168
        Paul McCartney & Michael Jackson
  126   Rock With You......................Epic 50797
  184   Beat It ....Epic 03759
  413   Man In The Mirror ....Epic 07668
  486   Bad ....Epic 07418
  667   Ben ....Motown 1207
  718   The Way You Make Me Feel .....Epic 07645
  729   Don't Stop 'Til You Get Enough ..Epic 50742
  746   I Just Can't Stop Loving You .....Epic 07253
  768   Dirty Diana ....Epic 07739

  834   The Girl Is Mine....................Epic 03288
        Michael Jackson/Paul McCartney
  930   Rockin' Robin...................Motown 1197
JACKSON 5, The
  65   I'll Be There ....Motown 1171
  350   ABC ....Motown 1163
  351   The Love You Save ....Motown 1166
  536   I Want You Back ....Motown 1157
  862   Never Can Say Goodbye ....Motown 1179
  898   Dancing Machine.................Motown 1286
JAMES, Sonny
  498   Young Love ....Capitol 3602
JAMES, Tommy, And The Shondells
  296   Crimson And Clover ....Roulette 7028
  480   Hanky Panky ....Roulette 4686
  842   Crystal Blue Persuasion ....Roulette 7050
JAN & DEAN
  426   Surf City ....Liberty 55580
JAYNETTS, The
  991   Sally, Go 'Round The Roses........Tuff 369
JEFFERSON STARSHIP - see STARSHIP
JETT, Joan, & The Blackhearts
  24   I Love Rock 'N Roll............Boardwalk 135
JOEL, Billy
  291   It's Still Rock And Roll To
        Me ....Columbia 11276
  368   We Didn't Start The Fire .....Columbia 73021
  612   Tell Her About It ....Columbia 04012
JOHN, Elton
  146   Don't Go Breaking My Heart ..Rocket 40585
        Elton John And Kiki Dee
  204   Crocodile Rock ....MCA 40000
  261   Island Girl.........................MCA 40461
  320   Philadelphia Freedom ....MCA 40364
  477   Lucy In The Sky With
        Diamonds ....MCA 40344
  537   Bennie And The Jets ....MCA 40198
  855   Goodbye Yellow Brick Road .....MCA 40148
JOHN, Robert
  526   Sad Eyes ....EMI America 8015
JOHNNY HATES JAZZ
  869   Shattered Dreams ....Virgin 99383
JOPLIN, Janis
  385   Me And Bobby McGee ....Columbia 45314
JOURNEY
  788   Open Arms ....Columbia 02687

K

KAEMPFERT, Bert
  191   Wonderland By Night ....Decca 31141
KC And The SUNSHINE BAND
  338   That's The Way (I Like It).........T.K. 1015
  505   Please Don't Go ....................T.K. 1035
  507   (Shake, Shake, Shake) Shake Your
        Booty ..............................T.K. 1019
  685   I'm Your Boogie Man ..............T.K. 1022
  782   Get Down Tonight .................T.K. 1009
  854   Keep It Comin' Love ...............T.K. 1023

100

the Hits

the Label

COLGEMS

66-1001

The Monkees

LAST TRAIN TO CLARKSVILLE / TAKE A GIANT STEP

Manufactured and Distributed by RCA

The Monkees!

Meet The Monkees...
A different-sounding new group with a live, infectious feeling demonstrated by a strong rock beat that generates excitement from the opening note to the last groove.
See the Screen Gems TV Show "The Monkees," produced by Bert Schneider and Robert Rafelson, every Monday night on NBC-TV at 7:30 pm E.D.T. beginning Sept. 12th.
"Last Train to Clarksville" produced by Tommy Boyce, and Bobby Hart. "Take A Giant Step" produced by Tommy Boyce, Bobby Hart and Jack Keller.

Music Supervisor Don Kirshner.

COLGEMS
Manufactured and Distributed by RCA

ORDER FROM YOUR RCA VICTOR DISTRIBUTOR TODAY!

O'SULLIVAN, Gilbert
  49   Alone Again (Naturally)...........MAM 3619
  942 Clair ....MAM 3626

P

PAGE, Patti
  886 Allegheny Moon ....Mercury 70878
PAGE, Tommy
  763 I'll Be Your Everything............Sire 19959
PALMER, Robert
  615 Addicted To Love.................Island 99570
  968 Simply Irresistible..............EMI-Man. 50133
PAPER LACE
  743 The Night Chicago Died ....Mercury 73492
PARKER, Ray Jr.
  193 Ghostbusters......................Arista 9212
PARR, John
  404 St. Elmo's Fire (Man In
        Motion) ....Atlantic 89541
PARTON, Dolly
  288 Islands In The Stream ....RCA 13615
        Kenny Rogers & Dolly Parton
  315 9 To 5 ....RCA 12133
PARTRIDGE FAMILY, The
  179 I Think I Love You ....Bell 910
PAUL, Billy
  222 Me And Mrs. Jones ....Phil. Int. 3521
PAUL & PAULA
  211 Hey Paula ....Philips 40084
PEACHES & HERB
  115 Reunited ....Polydor 14547
PEBBLES
  999 Mercedes Boy ....MCA 53279
PERKINS, Carl
  799 Blue Suede Shoes.....................Sun 234
PETER & GORDON
  599 A World Without Love..........Capitol 5175
PETER, PAUL and MARY
  518 Leaving On A Jet Plane ....Warner 7340
PET SHOP BOYS
  620 West End Girls ....EMI America 8307
  994 What Have I Done To Deserve
        This? ....EMI-Man. 50107
        Pet Shop Boys With Dusty Springfield
PHILLIPS, Phil, with The Twilights
  969 Sea Of Love ....Mercury 71465
PICKETT, Bobby 'Boris', & The Crypt-Kickers
  357 Monster Mash...................Garpax 44167
PINK FLOYD
  100 Another Brick In The Wall (Part
        II)..............................Columbia 11187
PLATTERS, The
  58   My Prayer.......................Mercury 70893
  189 Smoke Gets In Your Eyes......Mercury 71383
  285 The Great Pretender...........Mercury 70753
  504 Twilight Time...................Mercury 71289
PLAYER
  186 Baby Come Back ....RSO 879

POINTER SISTERS
  826 Slow Hand ....Planet 47929
  908 Fire.................................Planet 45901
POISON
  219 Every Rose Has Its Thorn ......Enigma 44203
POLICE, The
  15   Every Breath You Take ....A&M 2542
POPPY FAMILY featuring Susan Jacks
  996 Which Way You Goin' Billy?.....London 129
PRADO, Perez
  491 Patricia..............................RCA 7245
PRESLEY, Elvis
  1   Don't Be Cruel/Hound Dog ....RCA 6604
  6   All Shook Up.......................RCA 6870
  14   Heartbreak Hotel ....RCA 6420
  19   Jailhouse Rock ....RCA 7035
  20   (Let Me Be Your) Teddy Bear .....RCA 7000
  51   Are You Lonesome To-night? .....RCA 7810
  57   Love Me Tender ....RCA 6643
  63   It's Now Or Never ....RCA 7777
  69   Don't ....RCA 7150
  122 Stuck On You ....RCA 7740
  205 Too Much...........................RCA 6800
  392 Surrender ....RCA 7850
  425 Good Luck Charm ....RCA 7992
  431 A Big Hunk O' Love ....RCA 7600
  453 Hard Headed Woman...........RCA 7280
  495 I Want You, I Need You, I Love
        You ....RCA 6540
  725 Suspicious Minds ....RCA 9764
  792 Return To Sender...................RCA 8100
  895 Love Me ....RCA 992
PRESTON, Billy
  372 Will It Go Round In Circles........A&M 1411
  626 Nothing From Nothing............A&M 1544
PRESTON, Johnny
  192 Running Bear ....Mercury 71474
PRICE, Lloyd
  117 Stagger Lee ....ABC-Para. 9972
  833 Personality ....ABC-Para. 10018
PRINCE
  62   When Doves Cry.................Warner 29286
  330 Let's Go Crazy ....Warner 29216
  409 Kiss ....Paisley P. 28751
  742 Batdance ....Warner 22924
  953 Purple Rain ....Warner 29174
PUCKETT, Gary, & The Union Gap
  848 Young Girl ....Columbia 44450
  986 Lady Willpower ....Columbia 44547

Q

QUEEN
  105 Crazy Little Thing Called
        Love ....Elektra 46579
  165 Another One Bites The Dust ...Elektra 47031
? (QUESTION MARK) & THE MYSTERIANS
  555 96 Tears ....Cameo 428

106

R

RABBITT, Eddie
314 I Love A Rainy Night ....Elektra 47066
RAFFERTY, Gerry
789 Baker Street...................United Art. 1192
RAIDERS
540 Indian Reservation............Columbia 45332
RASCALS, The - see YOUNG RASCALS, The
RAWLS, Lou
916 You'll Never Find Another Love Like
      Mine ....Phil. Int. 3592
READY FOR THE WORLD
712 Oh Sheila...........................MCA 52636
REDDING, Otis
110 (Sittin' On) The Dock Of The Bay..Volt 157
REDDY, Helen
579 I Am Woman ....Capitol 3350
582 Delta Dawn ....Capitol 3645
719 Angie Baby.......................Capitol 3972
REEVES, Jim
823 He'll Have To Go ....RCA 7643
REO SPEEDWAGON
220 Can't Fight This Feeling ....Epic 04713
524 Keep On Loving You..............Epic 50953
REVERE, Paul - see RAIDERS
REYNOLDS, Debbie
56 Tammy...........................Coral 61851
RHYTHM HERITAGE
727 Theme From S.W.A.T..............ABC 12135
RICH, Charlie
436 The Most Beautiful Girl...........Epic 11040
RICHIE, Lionel
9 Endless Love.....................Motown 1519
      Diana Ross & Lionel Richie
97 All Night Long (All Night) .....Motown 1698
128 Say You, Say Me.................Motown 1819
301 Hello ....Motown 1722
311 Truly ....Motown 1644
915 Dancing On The Ceiling........Motown 1843
RIDDLE, Nelson
90 Lisbon Antigua ....Capitol 3287
RIGHTEOUS BROTHERS, The
241 (You're My) Soul And
      Inspiration ....Verve 10383
337 You've Lost That Lovin' Feelin' ..Philles 124
RILEY, Jeannie C.
557 Harper Valley P.T.A. ....Plantation 3
RIPERTON, Minnie
589 Lovin' You ....Epic 50057
RIVERS, Johnny
658 Poor Side Of Town ....Imperial 66205
990 Memphis ....Imperial 66032
ROBBINS, Marty
325 El Paso ....Columbia 41511
ROBINSON, Smokey
Also see The Miracles.

832 Being With You ....Tamla 54321
ROCKWELL
846 Somebody's Watching Me ......Motown 1702
RODGERS, Jimmie
94 Honeycomb ....Roulette 4015
ROE, Tommy
135 Dizzy ....ABC 11164
474 Sheila ....ABC-Para. 10329
ROGERS, Kenny
39 Lady................................Liberty 1380
288 Islands In The Stream ....RCA 13615
      Kenny Rogers & Dolly Parton
ROLLING STONES, The
111 Honky Tonk Women ....London 910
140 (I Can't Get No) Satisfaction....London 9766
389 Brown Sugar ....Rolling S. 19100
435 Paint It, Black ....London 901
476 Get Off Of My Cloud............London 9792
535 Miss You.......................Rolling S. 19307
646 Angie...........................Rolling S. 19105
681 Ruby Tuesday ....London 904
825 Start Me Up ....Rolling S. 21003
878 19th Nervous Breakdown ......London 9823
RONETTES, The
877 Be My Baby........................Philles 116
RONSTADT, Linda
770 You're No Good ....Capitol 3990
906 Don't Know Much ....Elektra 69261
      Linda Ronstadt (Featuring Aaron Neville)
945 When Will I Be Loved ....Capitol 4050
ROOFTOP SINGERS, The
428 Walk Right In ....Vanguard 35017
ROSE, David
551 The Stripper ....MGM 13064
ROSE ROYCE
545 Car Wash ....MCA 40615
ROSS, Diana
Also see The Supremes.
9 Endless Love.....................Motown 1519
      Diana Ross & Lionel Richie
93 Upside Down ....Motown 1494
209 Ain't No Mountain High
      Enough ....Motown 1169
334 Love Hangover ....Motown 1392
564 Touch Me In The Morning......Motown 1239
645 Theme From Mahogany (Do You Know
      Where You're Going To)......Motown 1377
ROXETTE
318 It Must Have Been Love..........EMI 50283
638 The Look ....EMI 50190
699 Listen To Your Heart..............EMI 50223
993 Dangerous ....EMI 50233
ROYAL GUARDSMEN, The
811 Snoopy Vs. The Red Baron.......Laurie 3366
RUBY & THE ROMANTICS
749 Our Day Will Come.................Kapp 501

S

T

974 Real Love ....MCA 53484
WEISSBERG, Eric, & Steve Mandell
816 Dueling Banjos ....Warner 7659
WELK, Lawrence
336 Calcutta ....Dot 16161
WELLS, Mary
379 My Guy.............................Motown 1056
WHAM! - see MICHAEL, George
WHITE, Barry
783 Can't Get Enough Of Your Love,
       Babe........................20th Century 2120
948 You're The First, The Last, My
       Everything.................20th Century 2133
WHITESNAKE
613 Here I Go Again.................Geffen 28339
WILD CHERRY
185 Play That Funky Music ....Epic 50225
WILDE, Kim
713 You Keep Me Hangin' On........MCA 53024
WILLIAMS, Andy
194 Butterfly...........................Cadence 1308
813 Can't Get Used To Losing
       You ....Columbia 42674
WILLIAMS, Deniece
329 Let's Hear It For The Boy ....Columbia 04417
597 Too Much, Too Little, Too
       Late...........................Columbia 10693
       Johnny Mathis/Deniece Williams
WILLIAMS, Mason
984 Classical Gas ....Warner 7190
WILLIAMS, Maurice, & The Zodiacs
758 Stay.................................Herald 552
WILLIAMS, Roger
89 Autumn Leaves......................Kapp 116
WILL TO POWER
689 Baby, I Love Your Way/Freebird Medley
       (Free Baby).......................Epic 08034
WILSON, Al
603 Show And Tell ....Rocky Road 30073
WILSON PHILLIPS
399 Release Me ....SBK 07327
528 Hold On...........................SBK 07322
WINGS - see McCARTNEY, Paul
WINTER, Edgar, Group
623 Frankenstein.......................Epic 10967
WINTERHALTER, Hugo/Eddie Heywood
885 Canadian Sunset....................RCA 6537

WINWOOD, Steve
156 Roll With It ....Virgin 99326
698 Higher Love.......................Island 28710
WITHERS, Bill
251 Lean On Me ....Sussex 235
827 Just The Two Of Us ....Elektra 47103
       Grover Washington, Jr. With Bill Withers
WONDER, Stevie
25 Ebony And Ivory...............Columbia 02860
       Paul McCartney With Stevie Wonder
190 I Just Called To Say I Love
       You...............................Motown 1745
228 Sir Duke...........................Tamla 54281
262 Fingertips - Pt 2 ....Tamla 54080
576 I Wish ....Tamla 54274
581 Part-Time Lover ....Tamla 1808
624 You Haven't Done Nothin ......Tamla 54252
643 You Are The Sunshine Of My
       Life...............................Tamla 54232
722 Superstition.......................Tamla 54226
929 For Once In My Life...............Tamla 54174
947 I Was Made To Love Her ......Tamla 54151
WOOLEY, Sheb
52 The Purple People Eater.........MGM 12651
WRIGHT, Gary
844 Dream Weaver ....Warner 8167
931 Love Is Alive ....Warner 8143

Y

YES
302 Owner Of A Lonely Heart ....Atco 99817
YOUNG, Neil
593 Heart Of Gold ....Reprise 1065
YOUNG, Paul
566 Everytime You Go Away .....Columbia 04867
YOUNG RASCALS, The
83 People Got To Be Free ....Atlantic 2537
       shown as: The Rascals
144 Groovin' ....Atlantic 2401
663 Good Lovin' ....Atlantic 2321

Z

ZAGER & EVANS
55 In The Year 2525 (Exordium &
       Terminus).........................RCA 0174

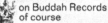

THE SONGS

This section lists, alphabetically, all titles listed in the *Top 1000* ranking. Listed next to each title is its final ranking in the *Top 1000*.

A song with more than one charted version is listed once, with the artist's names listed below it in rank order. Songs that have the same title, but are different tunes, are listed separately, with the highest ranked song listed first.

A

B

799 **Blue Suede Shoes** *Carl Perkins*
234 **Blue Velvet** *Bobby Vinton*
819 **Blueberry Hill** *Fats Domino*
850 **Boll Weevil Song** *Brook Benton*
971 **Boogie Down** *Eddie Kendricks*
609 **Boogie Fever** *Sylvers*
896 **Boogie Nights** *Heatwave*
173 **Boogie Oogie Oogie** *A Taste Of Honey*
872 **Born To Be Wild** *Steppenwolf*
861 **Boy Named Sue** *Johnny Cash*
195 **Brand New Key** *Melanie*
521 **Brandy (You're A Fine Girl)**
    Looking Glass
959 **Bread And Butter** *Newbeats*
421 **Breaking Up Is Hard To Do**
    Neil Sedaka
53 **Bridge Over Troubled Water**
    Simon & Garfunkel
902 **Bristol Stomp** *Dovells*
327 **Broken Wings** *Mr. Mister*
369 **Brother Louie** *Stories*
389 **Brown Sugar** *Rolling Stones*
964 **Burning Heart** *Survivor*
Butterfly
194   *Andy Williams*
376   *Charlie Gracie*
797 **Bye Bye Love** *Everly Brothers*

C

934 **C'est La Vie** *Robbie Nevil*
336 **Calcutta** *Lawrence Welk*
44 **Call Me** *Blondie*
817 **Calypso** *John Denver*
88 **Can't Buy Me Love** *Beatles*
220 **Can't Fight This Feeling**
    REO Speedwagon
783 **Can't Get Enough Of Your Love, Babe**
    Barry White
813 **Can't Get Used To Losing You**
    Andy Williams
981 **Can't You Hear My Heartbeat**
    Herman's Hermits
885 **Canadian Sunset**
    Hugo Winterhalter/Eddie Heywood
246 **Candy Man** *Sammy Davis, Jr.*
545 **Car Wash** *Rose Royce*
199 **Careless Whisper** *Wham!*
396 **Caribbean Queen (No More Love On
    The Run)** *Billy Ocean*
730 **Cat's In The Cradle** *Harry Chapin*
503 **Catch A Falling Star** *Perry Como*
81 **Cathy's Clown** *Everly Brothers*
882 **Causing A Commotion** *Madonna*
395 **Celebration** *Kool & The Gang*
43 **Centerfold** *J. Geils Band*
918 **Chain Gang** *Sam Cooke*
960 **Chain Of Fools** *Aretha Franklin*
494 **Chances Are** *Johnny Mathis*

267 **Chapel Of Love** *Dixie Cups*
539 **Chariots Of Fire - Titles** *Vangelis*
851 **Charlie Brown** *Coasters*
276 **Cherish** *Association*
853 **Cherish** *Kool & The Gang*
998 **Cherish** *Madonna*
159 **Chipmunk Song** *Chipmunks*
980 **Cisco Kid** *War*
942 **Clair** *Gilbert O'Sullivan*
984 **Classical Gas** *Mason Williams*
Close To You see: (They Long To Be)
914 **Closer I Get To You**
    Roberta Flack with Donny Hathaway
570 **Cold Hearted** *Paula Abdul*
1000 **Come Back To Me** *Janet Jackson*
696 **Come On Eileen**
    Dexys Midnight Runners
346 **Come See About Me** *Supremes*
152 **Come Softly To Me** *Fleetwoods*
538 **Come Together** *Beatles*
178 **Coming Up (Live at Glasgow)**
    Paul McCartney
669 **Convoy** *C.W. McCall*
448 **Could've Been** *Tiffany*
630 **Cracklin' Rosie** *Neil Diamond*
546 **Crazy For You** *Madonna*
105 **Crazy Little Thing Called Love** *Queen*
296 **Crimson And Clover**
    Tommy James & The Shondells
204 **Crocodile Rock** *Elton John*
979 **Cry Like A Baby** *Box Tops*
842 **Crystal Blue Persuasion**
    Tommy James & The Shondells

D

648 **Da Doo Ron Ron** *Shaun Cassidy*
103 **Da Ya Think I'm Sexy?** *Rod Stewart*
805 **Dancing In The Dark** *Bruce Springsteen*
954 **Dancing In The Street**
    Martha & The Vandellas
898 **Dancing Machine** *Jackson 5*
915 **Dancing On The Ceiling** *Lionel Richie*
567 **Dancing Queen** *Abba*
993 **Dangerous** *Roxette*
737 **Dark Lady** *Cher*
961 **Daydream** *Lovin' Spoonful*
125 **Daydream Believer** *Monkees*
274 **December, 1963 (Oh, What a Night)**
    Four Seasons
879 **Dedicated To The One I Love**
    Mamas & The Papas
660 **Deep Purple**
    Nino Tempo & April Stevens
582 **Delta Dawn** *Helen Reddy*
997 **Devil Inside** *INXS*
500 **Diana** *Paul Anka*
992 **Did You Ever Have To Make Up Your
    Mind?** *Lovin' Spoonful*

119

688 **Wishing Well** *Terence Trent D'Arby*
171 **Witch Doctor** *David Seville*
381 **With A Little Luck** *Wings*
227 **With Or Without You** *U2*
133 **Without You** *Nilsson*
824 **Woman** *John Lennon*
174 **Woman In Love** *Barbra Streisand*
191 **Wonderland By Night** *Bert Kaempfert*
655 **Wooden Heart** *Joe Dowell*
901 **Wooly Bully**
　　　Sam The Sham & The Pharoahs
907 **Working My Way Back To You**
　　　(medley) *Spinners*
599 **World Without Love** *Peter & Gordon*
970 **Wreck Of The Edmund Fitzgerald**
　　　Gordon Lightfoot

Y

822 **Y.M.C.A.** *Village People*
544 **Yakety Yak** *Coasters*
 33 **Yellow Rose Of Texas** *Mitch Miller*
933 **Yes, I'm Ready** *Teri DeSario with K.C.*
160 **Yesterday** *Beatles*
765 **You Ain't Seen Nothing Yet**
　　　Bachman-Turner Overdrive
643 **You Are The Sunshine Of My Life**
　　　Stevie Wonder
944 **You Belong To The City** *Glenn Frey*
391 **You Can't Hurry Love** *Supremes*
307 **You Don't Bring Me Flowers**
　　　Barbra Streisand & Neil Diamond
558 **You Don't Have To Be A Star (To Be In My Show)**
　　　Marilyn McCoo & Billy Davis, Jr.
884 **You Don't Own Me** *Lesley Gore*

695 **You Give Love A Bad Name** *Bon Jovi*
624 **You Haven't Done Nothin**
　　　Stevie Wonder
　　　You Keep Me Hangin' On
479 　　*Supremes*
713 　　*Kim Wilde*
 4 **You Light Up My Life** *Debby Boone*
912 **You Make Me Feel Brand New**
　　　Stylistics
562 **You Make Me Feel Like Dancing**
　　　Leo Sayer
559 **You Needed Me** *Anne Murray*
169 **You Send Me** *Sam Cooke*
649 **You Should Be Dancing** *Bee Gees*
916 **You'll Never Find Another Love Like Mine** *Lou Rawls*
278 **(You're) Having My Baby** *Paul Anka*
241 **(You're My) Soul And Inspiration**
　　　Righteous Brothers
770 **You're No Good** *Linda Ronstadt*
656 **You're Sixteen** *Ringo Starr*
182 **You're So Vain** *Carly Simon*
948 **You're The First, The Last, My Everything** *Barry White*
531 **You're The One That I Want**
　　　John Travolta & Olivia Newton-John
596 **You've Got A Friend** *James Taylor*
337 **You've Lost That Lovin' Feelin'**
　　　Righteous Brothers
876 **You've Made Me So Very Happy**
　　　Blood, Sweat & Tears
848 **Young Girl** *Union Gap*
　　　Young Love
 42 　　*Tab Hunter*
498 　　*Sonny James*

THE WHO

PINBALL WIZARD

Stereo 732465

FROM THE SOON TO BE RELEASED ROCK OPERA "TOMMY (1914/1984)"

b/w

"DOGS part II"

A Division of MCA, Inc.

MISCELLANEOUS

THE TOP 50 ARTISTS OF THE *TOP 1000*

RANK	TOP 1000		RANK	TOP 1000	
1)	21	The Beatles	26)	5	Olivia Newton-John
2)	19	Elvis Presley	27)	5	Prince
3)	14	The Supremes	28)	5	Paul Anka
4)	13	Michael Jackson	29)	5	Janet Jackson
5)	11	Paul McCartney/Wings	30)	5	The Temptations
6)	11	Stevie Wonder	31)	5	John Denver
7)	11	Madonna	32)	4	The Platters
8)	10	The Rolling Stones	33)	4	Bobby Vinton
9)	9	Bee Gees	34)	4	Paula Abdul
10)	8	George Michael/Wham!	35)	4	Blondie
11)	8	Phil Collins	36)	4	Marvin Gaye
12)	7	Daryl Hall & John Oates	37)	4	Sly & The Family Stone
13)	7	Elton John	38)	4	Roberta Flack
14)	7	Whitney Houston	39)	4	Bon Jovi
15)	7	KC & The Sunshine Band	40)	4	The Beach Boys
16)	7	Carpenters	41)	4	George Harrison
17)	6	Pat Boone	42)	4	Connie Francis
18)	6	Lionel Richie	43)	4	Neil Diamond
19)	6	Diana Ross	44)	4	Steve Miller Band
20)	6	Donna Summer	45)	4	Roxette
21)	6	The Jackson 5	46)	4	Richard Marx
22)	6	Eagles	47)	4	Aretha Franklin
23)	5	The 4 Seasons	48)	3	Rod Stewart
24)	5	Barbra Streisand	49)	3	Andy Gibb
25)	5	The Everly Brothers	50)	3	Dawn/Tony Orlando

Top 1000: Artist's total records making the *Top 1000*.

For artists with the same number of *Top 1000* hits, ties are broken by totaling the final ranking of each *Top 1000* hit by these artists, and the artist with the highest ranking is listed first, and so on.

SONGS WITH MORE THAN ONE HIT VERSION
Peak Position/Year (*Top 1000* Rank)

1. **Young Love**
   Tab Hunter   1/'57 (42)
   Sonny James   1/'57 (498)

2. **Go Away Little Girl**
   Donny Osmond   1/'71 (207)
   Steve Lawrence   1/'63 (348)

3. **Butterfly**
   Andy Williams   1/'57 (194)
   Charlie Gracie   1/'57 (376)

4. **Lean On Me**
   Bill Withers   1/'72 (251)
   Club Nouveau   1/'87 (470)

5. **The Loco-Motion**
   Grand Funk   1/'74 (447)
   Little Eva   1/'62 (654)

6. **You Keep Me Hangin' On**
   The Supremes   1/'66 (479)
   Kim Wilde   1/'87 (713)

7. **Venus**
   The Shocking Blue   1/'70 (553)
   Bananarama   1/'86 (650)

8. **Please Mr. Postman**
   The Marvelettes   1/'61 (607)
   Carpenters   1/'75 (766)

9. **I Heard It Through The Grapevine**
   Marvin Gaye   1/'68 (29)
   Gladys Knight & The Pips   2/'67 (841)

10. **Rockin' Robin**
    Bobby Day   2/'58 (889)
    Michael Jackson   2/'72 (930)

SAME TITLES — DIFFERENT SONGS

The following *Top 1000* songs have the same title, but are not by the same composer(s). The artist with the highest ranked version is listed first, along with the year the record peaked.

Best Of My Love
Emotions ('77)
The Eagles ('75)

Cherish
The Association ('66)
Kool & The Gang ('85)
Madonna ('89)

Fire
Ohio Players ('75)
Pointer Sisters ('79)
The Crazy World Of
   Arthur Brown ('68)

Heaven
Bryan Adams ('85)
Warrant ('89)

I'm Sorry
Brenda Lee ('60)
John Denver ('75)

My Love
Paul McCartney & Wings ('73)
Petula Clark ('66)

Venus
Frankie Avalon ('59)
The Shocking Blue ('70) and
   Bananarama ('86)

RE-CHARTED SINGLES

The *Top 1000* singles which hit the charts more than once.

RANK   **Peak Position/Year(Weeks Charted)**

11) **Rock Around The Clock**...*Bill Haley & His Comets*
1/'55(24); 39/'74(14)

12) **The Wayward Wind**...*Gogi Grant*
1/'56(28); 50/'61(9)

61) **All I Have To Do Is Dream**...*The Everly Brothers*
1/'58(17); 96/'61(2)

125) **Daydream Believer**...*The Monkees*
1/'67(12); 79/'86(4)

137) **Ode To Billie Joe**...*Bobbie Gentry*
1/'67(14); 54/'76(6)

159) **The Chipmunk Song**...*The Chipmunks*
1/'58(13); 41/'59(5); 45/'60(3); 39/'61(3); 40/'62(4)

161) **The Twist**...*Chubby Checker*
1/'60(18); 1/'62(21)

202) **Light My Fire**...*The Doors*
1/'67(17); 87/'68(6)

357) **Monster Mash**...*Bobby "Boris" Pickett & The Crypt-Kickers*
1/'62(14); 91/'70(3); 10/'73(20)

438) **At This Moment**...*Billy Vera & The Beaters*
79/'81(3); 1/'87(21)

487) **I Honestly Love You**...*Olivia Newton-John*
1/'74(15); 48/'77(9)

684) **Red Red Wine**...*UB40*
34/'84(15); 1/'88(25)

759) **When I'm With You**...*Sheriff*
61/'83(7); 1/'89(21)

790) **Louie Louie**...*The Kingsmen*
2/'63(16); 97/'66(2)

812) **Twist And Shout**...*The Beatles*
2/'64(11); 23/'86(15)

818) **Honky Tonk**...*Bill Doggett*
2/'56(29); 57/'61(10)

879) **Dedicated To The One I Love**...*The Shirelles*
83/'59(4); 3/'61(16)

BREAKDOWN BY YEAR

Total records making the *Top 1000* year-by-year.

YR	TOP 1000			YR	TOP 1000	
55	9			70	24	
56	22			71	24	
57	26			72	28	
58	29			73	34	
59	23			74	39	
Total	**109**	(11%)		75	40	
				76	36	
				77	34	
				78	23	
				79	28	
				Total	**310**	(31%)

YR	TOP 1000			YR	TOP 1000	
60	24			80	22	
61	25			81	26	
62	24			82	21	
63	26			83	23	
64	28			84	24	
65	28			85	32	
66	34			86	35	
67	27			87	32	
68	25			88	39	
69	26			89	37	
Total	**267**	(27%)		**Total**	**291**	(29%)

YR	TOP 1000	
90	23	
Total	**23**	(2%)

JOEL WHITBURN:
THE ALL-TIME RECORD HOLDER

If Joel Whitburn ever invites you over to listen to records, plan on spending several months.

That's about how long it would take to spin through all of the 60,000 or so singles in Joel's collection — back to back with *no* breaks. (Take a few turns through Joel's 40,000+ albums, and you can figure on adding years to your listening time.)

Along the way, you'll hear every hit that ever made the *Hot 100*. It's quite an earful — but that's what it takes to compile books such as *Top 1000 Singles* and the many other volumes published by Joel's Record Research firm.

From a few handwritten chart statistics jotted on file cards over two decades ago, to the vast computerized data base of chart information he now commands, Joel Whitburn has firmly established himself as *the* single most reliable source for facts and figures on the music people listen to and love.

With over fifty books published to date by his Record Research firm, Joel has detailed the history and development of charted music from 1890 to the present. His chart knowledge spans virtually every musical genre: from Rock 'n Roll to Easy Listening, from Pop to Country to Rhythm & Blues.

Today, Joel and his team of researchers dissect and analyze *Billboard's* charts in ever-greater depth and diversity, packing even more data and statistics into each new Record Research volume. The radio and music industries worldwide, along with countless collectors, musicologists, and other music enthusiasts, rely regularly on Joel's books for accurate, detailed chart information.

Joel's vast record library — the largest privately held collection in the world — completely fills an environmentally controlled underground vault adjacent to the Whitburn home in Menomonee Falls, Wisconsin. Included in the collection are all of the titles to ever appear on *Billboard's* Hot 100 and *Top Pop Albums* charts, along with many of the records that made all of the other *Billboard* charts.

THE BILLBOARD CHARTS

Only Joel Whitburn's Record Research Books List Every Record To Ever Appear On Every Major Billboard Chart.

When the talk turns to music, more people turn to Joel Whitburn's Record Research Collection than to any other reference source.

That's because these are the only books that get right to the bottom of Billboard's major charts, with **complete, fully accurate chart data on every record ever charted.** So they're quoted with confidence by DJ's, music show hosts, program directors, collectors and other music enthusiasts worldwide.

Each book lists every record's significant chart data, such as peak position, debut date, peak date, weeks charted, label, record number and much more, all conveniently arranged for fast, easy reference. Most books also feature artist biographies, record notes, RIAA Platinum/Gold Record certifications, top artist and record achievements, all-time artist and record rankings, a chronological listing of all #1 hits, and additional in-depth chart information.

And now, the new large-format **Billboard Hot 100 Charts** book series takes chart research one step further, by actually reproducing weekly "Hot 100" charts by decade.

Joel Whitburn's Record Research Collection. #1 on **everyone's** hit list.

THE BILLBOARD HOT 100 CHARTS:
THE SIXTIES 1960-1969
THE SEVENTIES 1970-1979
Two complete collections of all 520 actual "Hot 100" charts from each decade, reproduced in black-and-white at 70% of original size. Deluxe Hardcover. $90.00 each.

TOP POP ALBUMS 1955-1985
The 14,000 LPs that ever appeared on *Billboard's* Pop albums charts, arranged by artist. Softcover. $50.00.

TOP POP SINGLES 1955-1990
20,000 Pop singles - every "Hot 100" hit - arranged by artist. $70.00 Hardcover/$60.00 Softcover.

POP SINGLES ANNUAL 1955-1990
A year-by-year ranking, based on chart performance, of 20,000 "Hot 100" singles. $70.00 Hardcover/$60.00 Softcover.

POP MEMORIES 1890-1954
The only documented chart history of early American popular music, arranged by artist. $60.00 Hardcover/$50.00 Softcover.

FROM TOP TO BOTTOM!

TOP COUNTRY SINGLES 1944-1988
An artist-by-artist listing of every "Country" single ever charted. $60.00 Hardcover/$50.00 Softcover.

TOP R&B SINGLES 1942-1988
Every "Soul," "Black," "Urban Contemporary" and "Rhythm & Blues" charted single, listed by artist. $60.00 Hardcover/$50.00 Softcover.

BILLBOARD'S TOP 10 CHARTS 1958-1988
1,550 actual, weekly Top 10 Pop singles charts in the original "Hot 100" chart format. $60.00 Hardcover/$50.00 Softcover.

BUBBLING UNDER THE HOT 100 1959-1981
Over 4,000 big regional hits, one-shot efforts and other semi-popular singles from the "Bubbling Under" Pop charts, arranged by artist. Softcover. $35.00.

BILLBOARD'S TOP 3000+ 1955-1990
Every single that ever appeared in the Top 10 of *Billboard's* Pop charts, ranked by all-time popularity. Softcover. $40.00.

MUSIC YEARBOOKS 1983/1984/1985/1986
The complete story of each year in music, covering *Billboard's* biggest singles and albums charts. Softcover. $35.00 each.

MUSIC & VIDEO YEARBOOKS 1987/1988/1989
Comprehensive, yearly updates on *Billboard's* major singles, albums and videocassettes charts. Softcover. $35.00 each.

DAILY #1 HITS 1940-1989
A day-by-day listing of the #1 Pop records of the past 50 years. Spiral-bound softcover. $25.00.

For complete book descriptions and ordering information, call, write or fax today.

Record Research
The World's Leading Authority
On Recorded Entertainment

RECORD RESEARCH INC.
P.O. Box 200
Menomonee Falls, WI 53052-0200
Phone 414-251-5408
Fax 414-251-9452